"Most investors miss opportunities in new markets simply because they are unaware of them. Asha will tell you how to make money in these markets before they have even emerged."

—**JIM ROGERS,** International Investor & Author of *Street Smarts*

"Asha Mehta demonstrates not only why we need to invest in women, but also how our industry benefits from the combination of analytical rigor and global understanding of human behavior that women investors, like Asha, bring to the table."

—**AMANDA PULLINGER,** CEO of 100 Women in Finance

"Asha Mehta provides a powerful exposition of how our global sustainability challenges are also the biggest opportunities for capital markets to fund the needed solutions."

—**GEORGE SERAFEIM,** Award-Winning Scholar, Harvard Business School

"A most enjoyable and fascinating book by a pioneer in sustainable finance in emerging market economies. It is a firsthand account of her journeys through some of the hottest and, sometimes most controversial, emerging markets, how she learned to operate and invest successfully in them, and ultimately how private capital can help fight climate change."

—**HARINDER KOHLI,** Former Director, World Bank; Founding Director and Chief Executive, Emerging Markets Forum

"In her epic journey across the globe, Asha Mehta gives us a brave and bold analysis of the breathtaking challenges reshaping our world. Her journey from UP to the UN is truly inspirational. She has knitted together the interplay of financial returns, sustainability, the empowerment of women in the workplace and society and the role of technology in a succinct manner. The book shows how far society has come, but also how much more there is to do. She presents a vision that investors and business leaders alike should consider."

—**VIJAY ADVANI,** Former CEO of TIAA / Nuveen, Board Member of the Global Impact Investing Network

"A revolution is occurring in the emerging world. Geopolitics, technology, and sustainability are upending the established order. Provocative and pioneering, Asha Mehta's *Power of Capital* will help you make sense of it all."

—**SELORM ADADEVOH,** CEO of
MTN Ghana

"This book tells the story of a headstrong young woman traveling the world with deep confidence, sensitivity, and insight. From traveling in India with no male chaperone, to Saudi Arabia with no head covering, she makes it all look easy. The resulting insights into investment opportunities in these emerging and frontier markets, backed up by real and innovative quantitative tools, give her a unique and distinctive perspective on the world. This is a book you will not want to miss, nor put down once you pick it up."

—**CHURCHILL FRANKLIN,** Co-Founder and
CEO Emeritus, Acadian; Executive Chair, Intech

"We live in an era of unremitting geopolitical crises alongside vast institutional wealth. Optimistic and perceptive, *Power of Capital* reveals the opportunity to build a sustainable ecosystem that we dare not waste."

—**AJMAL AHMADY,** Former Governor
of the Afghanistan Central Bank

POWER
OF CAPITAL

POWER OF CAPITAL

AN ADVENTURE CAPITALIST'S JOURNEY TO A SUSTAINABLE FUTURE

ASHA MEHTA

WILEY

Published by John Wiley & Sons, Inc., Hoboken, New Jersey.
Published simultaneously in Canada.

For general information on our other products and services or for technical support, please contact our Customer Care Department within the United States at (800) 762-2974, outside the United States at (317) 572-3993 or fax (317) 572-4002.

Wiley also publishes its books in a variety of electronic formats. Some content that appears in print may not be available in electronic formats. For more information about Wiley products, visit our web site at www.wiley.com.

Library of Congress Cataloging-in-Publication Data:

Names: Mehta, Asha, 1978- author.
Title: Power of capital : an adventure capitalist's journey to a sustainable
  future / Asha Mehta.
Description: First Edition. | Hoboken, New Jersey : Wiley, [2023] |
  Includes index.
Identifiers: LCCN 2022013194 (print) | LCCN 2022013195 (ebook) | ISBN
  9781119906032 (cloth) | ISBN 9781119906056 (adobe pdf) | ISBN
  9781119906049 (epub)
Subjects: LCSH: China—Commerce. | Developing countries—Commerce. |
  Capitalism—China. | Capitalism—Developing countries.
Classification: LCC HF3836.5 (print) | LCC HF3836.5 (ebook) | DDC
  795.8/4—dc24/eng/20220437
LC record available at https://lccn.loc.gov/2022013194
LC ebook record available at https://lccn.loc.gov/2022013195

Cover Design: Wiley
Cover Image: © ipopba/Getty Images

SKY10035962_091322

Power of Capital *is dedicated to*
my father, who inspired me to travel;
my mother, who taught me to marvel;
my husband and our world tours;
and my children—the future is yours.

Contents

Adventure Capital: An Introduction

Before I became an international investor, I intended to become a doctor. While I was premed at Stanford in the late 1990s, I decided to field-test my dream of serving the impoverished. I told my father that I was going to India—the same place he had escaped after fleeing the massacres during the Partition and growing up in a refugee camp without running water.

"Asha," he lamented, "you cannot imagine what you will see. The poor are poorer than you think."

Emboldened by my passion, I went, nonetheless. In Lucknow, a huge city in northern India, in one of the country's poorest states (Uttar Pradesh), I felt perceived as a renegade. In some ways, the city was a modern metropolis, but it was still governed by a very conservative culture. Women in pastel- and jewel-toned saris looked disapprovingly at my jeans and uncovered arms, taking rickshaws by myself with no male chaperone.

"*Iske lardke pagal hai,*" they would mutter. I worked out with my limited Hindi vocabulary what that meant: "She's a crazy girl." Men and young boys would unflinchingly ogle me as they sat beside me. I would just look away.

I was staying with a host family, and it was my intention to follow the father to his job at the hospital and shadow his work. By Indian standards, the hospital was a modern facility. The hospital administration was proud that they offered procedures as advanced as kidney transplants. But I wasn't in Palo Alto anymore. What I saw were chipped instruments, crumbling drywall, and bloodstains on the floors. This was a time when AIDS was running rampant through India, and my host father didn't even have gloves. He performed surgery with a scalpel in his bare hands that he had washed thoroughly with soap and water.

As he operated, my father's words ran through my head. He was right. I couldn't have ever imagined. Out in the waiting room, perched on the dilapidated furniture were the families of the patients. During rounds, I would catch a glimpse of them, wiping wet eyes. As I watched them in their tattered clothes, unbrushed hair, and holed shoes, I reached the conclusion that these people needed help long before they arrived at the hospital. I realized then and there I wasn't going to be a doctor. What these people needed was not *health*, but rather *wealth*.

Over the following quarter century, I built a career investing in emerging economies such as India. During this period, emerging economies have transformed in ways that many others can't imagine.

When asked simple questions about global trends—what percentage of the world's population live in poverty; why the world's population is increasing; how many girls finish school—people frequently get the answers wrong. Is development still about "banks, beer, and cement"? Not anymore. It's true that the successful emerging market countries started by playing by the Old Economy playbook. Central planning in the late 1900s set the stage, variously, for a commodities boom, a manufacturing-based economy, and/or an open-armed embrace of globalization.

The prosperity of many emerging-market countries has risen dramatically in the past 20 years. The rapid growth means that the world as a whole must be regarded through a different lens. Emerging markets should no longer be regarded as poor and disadvantaged. Rather, on some measures, they are on a fast track to overtake Western countries.

What Is an Emerging Market?

China has become the poster child for the changes underway in emerging markets. A mere 20 years ago, America was sending Peace Corps volunteers to China to help the struggling nation. Today, China accounts for 15% of the world's economy, and its contribution to global GDP growth now outpaces that of the United States.[1]

Established emerging countries, such as China, have become mainstream investments in the past 40 years. With increased access to technology, capital, and governance standards, these countries have evolved and grown, making for a dynamic, deep, and diversified group.

The biggest winner over the past decade is without a doubt Asia. Today, Asia comprises the vast majority of emerging countries' worth. They've achieved their success by elevating the consumer class and establishing themselves as the world's technological leaders. For instance, South Korean companies have become worldwide household names (think: LG electronics, Samsung, or Hyundai).

Outdated conceptions of "first-" and "third-world countries" are not only offensive today, but they are steeped in the antiquated inaccuracy of the "second-world countries" designation used for the old Communist Bloc. At one point, my former colleague Jim O'Neill at Goldman Sachs coined the term BRIC markets, or those in Brazil, Russia, India, and China. Yet that did not include more than 50 emerging market countries.

Today, classifications are largely based on established benchmarks. A "frontier" economy is ranked below an "emerging" economy. In general, they measure similar considerations, specifically those that relate to market openness. That's important: the classifications are not based on size, geopolitical importance, or the type of government. Rather, they examine the fundamental ability of investors to put capital to work. If a market is open and accessible, investors can invest with the confidence that the markets can be navigated with simplicity, that their holding rights will be respected, and that capital will be returned if called.

In fixed income, a country's classification directly affects the pricing of a sovereign bond. A country's cost of capital—its ability to borrow at reasonable rates—is also tied directly to its classification. At this point, only seven countries, all small by comparison, have been "upgraded" into the emerging markets classification over the past 15 years: Colombia, Qatar, United Arab Emirates (UAE), Pakistan, Morocco, Saudi Arabia, and Argentina. (The rest of the countries in the emerging markets classification were grandfathered in.)

In equities, it can be more about prestige. On a cold January morning in Boston, I hosted the chairman of the Pakistan Stock Exchange in my office. He was giddy with joy and pride that his stock exchange had just been upgraded. He beamed as he told me, "We became an emerging market before China!" I laughed out loud. No one could question which country was the Goliath.

Nevertheless, I shared in the chairman's joy; the upgrade from frontier to emerging generated substantial returns for investors like me. The upgrades can matter for equities, because when a country graduates into the emerging market asset class, significant-return events can occur. The inclusion marks the moment that a country goes from nearly uninvestable into the mainstream. As a result, a ton of capital crowds into the country, sending returns soaring. When the UAE joined the index, its stock market immediately doubled in size; from the time that the classification agency announced the upgrade to time that the change became effective, investors had the chance to double their money, as the market posted a cool 99% return in 12 months.

Power of Capital

Capturing a return like that can make an investor's career. And I sought to do it again in the next great Gulf market: Saudi Arabia. But conducting on-the-ground research in Riyadh wasn't easy. First, there was the awkward fact of being female. The strict limitations on interactions between men and women in Saudi seemed shocking at first. Just about everyone refused to look at me—a reflex that, tragically and comically, reminded me of my days at investment conferences back home in Boston, where women in attendance were rare!

Even approaching the Saudi Telecom Company (STC) headquarters for an investor meeting was an intimidating experience. The walled compound resembles a military fortress. Which, in a way, is appropriate. As a national security interest with significant state ownership, STC hosts sensitive state information.

As my entourage passed through the heavily barricaded steel front gates, our van was stopped by a guard asking for identification. My host, a broker, deftly fielded the man's questions in Arabic. The guard peered into our vehicle. We were a fine bunch, Westerners dressed in sleek dark gray and deep blue suits, holding briefcases, polished and prepared for our day of meetings. As the lone female, I stood out. My black abaya made me feel invisible and inexcusable, all at once.

Staring at me, the guard asked my broker why I was present. He told the man that I was a large investor evaluating STC. The guard said that I couldn't be admitted. My broker insisted that I had to be. And so it went. I could sense the growing tension as they spoke, even if I had no idea what was actually being said. After some aggressive back-and-forth, including a demand that I show my passport—I was the only one in the group obliged to do this—I was finally allowed to enter along with the others.

There wasn't another woman in sight. If the company had any female workers, they would be sequestered, required to work in a separate building. In this instance, I found that wearing an abaya embarrassed and emboldened me at once.

In the conference room, I peppered the management team with questions about its long-term objectives and liberalization outlook. The atmosphere was strained. The investor relations team relayed their facts to us in officialese: fully accurate but lacking in color. When questioned, they revealed almost nothing. Still, I had to credit them for trying—the very idea of an investor relations team was a revolutionary one for the Kingdom a decade ago. Clearly, the Saudis were evolving with the times.

And evolve they did. Over the following years, Saudi Arabia liberalized its market, allowing foreign capital. The country became the largest market to be included in the Emerging Markets index in history, and investors who were early to this market were well rewarded. When countries remove the barriers to global flows, foreign investments start pouring in. International investors caught on to this tidal shift and helped catalyze the change. That promoted the rise of a growing consumer class. Rapid liberalization has brought billions into the middle class. They position the emerging markets to surpass the standards of their developed market peers over the next decade.

Markets of the Gulf Cooperation Council (GCC), and Saudi Arabia in particular, constitute the most important investment story of the past decade. Investing in this region used to mean a simple bet on oil. That was before the country allowed foreign capital to enter, driving efficiency, transparency, and liquidity into the private sector. Liberalizing capital has not only enabled foreign capital to enter the Gulf markets, it has likewise allowed capital to exit. Today, the GCC sovereign wealth funds are among the largest pools of capital across the globe.

The Gulf's transformation from a desert, Bedouin land dotted with camels and oil rigs to a global financial epicenter with a thriving consumer class has lured deep-pocketed investors.

On the other hand, governments that have proven untrustworthy to promote free and open trade have slid back into irrelevance. That's why some shining stars among emerging market countries a decade ago, such as Russia and Turkey, have lost their luster. Argentina, once the cultural and economic capital of the Southern Cone with the same GDP as Canada, was recently demoted *below* an emerging market classification. The list goes on. Following an airstrike in Lebanon, all of the major institutional banks closed their offices in Beirut, locking out pools of capital. Instability reaches down, ultimately, into the lives of all of a country's citizens, suppressing innovation. For anyone trying to judge which country will rise, these indicator arrows are pointing straight down.

When stability and good governance arise, investors take note, seek growth, and allocate capital. Improving wealth builds a virtuous cycle of prosperity and investments. Colombia is a case example. In a taxicab in Bogota in 2003, my driver careened through the streets; when I asked him to slow, my driver matter-of-factly explained the risks of being stopped, robbed, kidnapped, and worse by drug traffickers. A few short years later, after Colombia ended its civil war and peace took over, the country's financial markets experienced the first ever "upgrade" from frontier to emerging market status. The country's returns soared, and Colombia became the first dramatic success story of my career.

Having shed their "banana republic" past with threats of military rule and desolate poverty, emerging markets today are the fastest growing, most dynamic markets across the globe.

Technology: AI for Alpha and Impact

Key among the drivers of the emerging markets' growth spurt is technology. The FinTech and telecom revolutions have enabled the rise of savings accounts, credit lending, and other financial tools that fuel business growth in these regions. Thanks to HealthTech, rural dwellers have more rapid access to medical care than ever before. As a result, lives have been saved and well-being improved.

Across the world, the rise of technology has been a growth phenomenon. Tech has given us speed, precision, robustness, and scale. It has liberated us from such disparate constraints as paper-based calculations, rows of workers, and national boundaries. Leveraging machines has brought great benefits in terms of objectivity, scalability, and cost.

I know. I have been a global quantitative investor for more than 20 years, using technology to cover tens of thousands of stocks and more technology to build portfolios with hundreds of stocks. This infrastructure has enabled me to invest capital in the farthest corners of the globe, in tiny increments that reach down in the poorest countries' penny stock companies, all because of technology.

The nature of the investment industry is not only upturned by tech, but it has been rewarded as well. The past decade's market returns have been dominated by tech: in the United States, it's been the FANG stocks (Facebook, Apple, Netflix, and Google), and in the emerging markets, the winners have been China's BATs (Baidu, Alibaba, and Tencent). The sector has so much redefined global economies that MSCI was obliged years ago to redefine its sector definitions to better account for technology.

Global as this change is, when it comes to emerging markets, the opportunity is outsized. Technology brings tangible advantages to leapfrog the developed world and to get emerging economies roaring.

For one, technology is cheap, which is essential for populations with less spending power. Over the past decade, as the cost of technology has plummeted, the number of smartphone owners has skyrocketed from 150 million to 4 billion. The population of more than half the world today carries a supercomputer in their pockets.

With this technology in hand and demographics on their side, emerging economies are innovating faster and better than their global peers. Around 90% of the world's population under 30 live in developing economies,[2] and this young cohort is quick to adapt to technology and eager to develop it further. The results speak for themselves: since 2017,[3] digital revenue in emerging markets has grown by an average of 26% per year, compared with 11% in developed countries.

Technology not only equalizes wealth across borders but within borders as well. Cell phone technology has empowered a revolution. I've spoken to a SIM seller in Brazil who obtained his street license by mobile phone, a day worker in Lagos who picks up jobs by phone rather than losing hours in traffic to visit his old job site, and my own elderly Auntie in Bhiwani, India, self-authenticates with optical biometrics to do her mobile banking. E-commerce has brought billions into the formal economy, lifting the poor, giving them voice, providing capital to the financially starved, and creating tax revenue for countries along the way.

What Does the Future Hold?

As technology and capital fuse together to create new sectors and reward innovators, investors often ask what for. Is growth inexorable in a depleting planet? Does technology deliver the cohesion we had envisioned? While the poor are poorer than we expect, why are the rich richer? Questions like these prompt businesses, citizens, and governments alike to consider how systemically interlinked each part of our economy is.

By 2010, investors globally began to recognize the power of their capital in generating a more sustainable world. By 2015, world leaders were ready to take action. The historic signing of the Paris Agreement holistically enacted a set of principles that have driven meaningful climate action. The largest emerging market economies, China and India, have become leaders in developing novel technologies that reduce the dependency on fossil fuels and hence reduce pollution, improve health, and mitigate unrest.

Socially and environmentally, while we are more interconnected than ever, the disparities between social classes had never been so stark.

As a result, the largest power center—the private sector—is taking action. Recognizing the possibilities for a more just world if power and capital were wielded by leaders who reflected its constituents, the capital markets have begun to embrace diversity, equity, and inclusion. Sustainable investing has gone mainstream, trillions of dollars are earmarked, and corporate leadership teams, compelled by their investors, are exhibiting their willingness to bend the future.

In May 2020, the most powerful US leaders, CEOs of the globe's largest multinational firms, signed the Business Roundtable Agreement. This statement redefined the role of capital in designing our societies. On the fiftieth anniversary of Milton Friedman's seminal statement that "the role of business in society is business," inequality and a multi-stakeholder approach instead took center focus.

The integration of the world's economic systems forces us to recognize that capital is the currency that builds ecosystems—from China's dominance to Russia's relevance to American's well-being. How we wield that capital enables us to generate not just tomorrow's return but also tomorrow's ecosystems.

In real time, we're witnessing awakened investors around the globe embrace the power of their capital to build tomorrow's ecosystems, ultimately, to generate returns for our investors while driving lasting positive impact through our investments.

As we set our allocation agendas, many adventure capitalists are leaning into the emerging markets where volatility can be hedged and returns can be made. The broader opportunity in emerging markets is especially profound. Not only are emerging markets high-growth, high-return markets, they also represent countries that face urgent environmental, political, and economic challenges. The UN Sustainable Development Goals (SDGs) unite capital allocators, from multilaterals and governments to private investors, to use their capital to address critical challenges, from poverty and inequality to climate change and environmental degradation. With a targeted goal of 2030, investors are pumping trillions of dollars into local economies as well as the required technologies.

Given the coming flood of sustainable assets, the rise of emerging markets, and access to technologies, the SDGs have the potential to reshape the global economy for the next 20 years.

While the developments in the future remain unknown, the overall patterns have emerged by now in full relief. Emerging markets began their modern economic journey with an industrial base, taking advantage of their cheap resources—both labor and commodities. But accessible and inexpensive technology has enabled them to leapfrog into the future. As better-educated, tech-enabled consumer classes have grown in these countries, they are poised today to vault upward. We can now bring vast sums of private investment capital to deliver both returns and positive social impact.

Today's lens toward a sustainable ecosystem highlights the fact that investments can help governments achieve social ambitions that improve the lives of millions of ordinary people.

When I returned to the villages in Uttar Pradesh, India, two decades after that fateful journey to the Lucknow hospitals, the landscape had shifted—quite literally. Farmers in the villages were by now on the cusp of adopting smart technology, far from the times when they relied on reading the clouds.

"I produce chili much faster and with less pain in my hands," one woman told me as I glanced at her hardened, thin fingers with thick, protruding knuckles. She went on to say that she now used the same amount of pesticide for a week that had previously lasted only for three days. In my mind's eye, I could picture the increased margins on her financial statement and what an influx of capital could do for her. She smiled a toothless grin at me and said, "Because I know now how much to use."

As her Indian village emerges onto my financial stage, we become a global village in real time. The power of capital—used responsibly to deliver both profits and purpose—can ensure that we all benefit alike.

1

What Is an Emerging Market?

China: The Opportunities and Risks Within the World's Second-Largest Economy

When I was 14, I traveled with my father to Shanghai. The last leg of our 36-hour journey was a midnight rickshaw ride. Pedaling us was a thin, barefoot teenager who spoke to us in Mandarin, which neither of us could understand.

Wiry and hard-faced with legs covered in dust, the pedaler looked only slightly older than me, and I wondered how he would get enough sleep before school the next day. Then it struck me: He didn't go to school. This was his life, realms away from mine. School was irrelevant to him.

A decade later, the gold-foil seal on my Wharton MBA degree was still fresh as I landed once again in Shanghai. Only this time I wasn't pulled around by a rickshaw on a dirt road. From the city's massive Pudong International Airport, I climbed into the brand-new magnetic levitation train, like a child on a theme-park ride. My stomach dropped as the train lifted off the tracks and began to float on air. The ride was silent and smooth with occasional wind hisses and ground roars as we glided through air at a blistering speed. When the train slid to a stop, I exited. I figured I'd find my way to my hotel from there.

I found myself amid a sea of restaurants, fruit stands, clothing stores, and two-yuan shops (25-cent shops). The words of the original adventure capitalist, Jim Rogers, echoed in my ears: "The Chinese are the best capitalists." Though I had perceived the country to be a beacon of communism, China's new commerce, competition, and energy were jarring.

I made my way to the hotel, nestled in the frenetic energy of the Pudong district, excited for the adventure ahead—a one-month journey through this emerging region. On my first evening, I marveled as hundreds of people emerged from surrounding high-rise apartments to convene on manicured courtyards and shopping center walkways.

In the Chinese courtyard, singles line-danced, and couples waltzed against the backdrop of luminous skyscrapers that housed families and businesses, often within the same complex. The skyscrapers were outlined with lights that beamed and blinked into meticulous designs. The streets hummed from the tires of Maseratis, e-bikes, and rickshaws that all paused as throngs of people filled the double-wide crosswalks. Seated next to a family chattering on a bench, I sipped mint tea and took it all in.

A mix of Western coffee shops' vanilla and chicory and old-world markets' sesame and garlic scented the streets and alleyways. Music blared from all around: stone-shaped stereos along shopping center sidewalks, booths in markets, and cyclists' Bluetooth speakers. Yet the myriad conversations in Mandarin, less Cantonese, and a bit of English among young students could not be drowned out by the music.

While I could see a richness in the culture, all of its potential, these markets were still hungry for wealth. The limited access to capital starved the local economy, the ability of businesses to thrive, and, in fact, for humans themselves to thrive. *With greater wealth,* I mused, *the local economy could soar, bringing prosperity and peace to these people.*

A quarter century has since passed. If economic dominance of the twentieth century was a race, the United States ran away with the gold. Even now it accounts for a quarter of the global economy. However, while the United States is squarely positioned as the world's principal financial powerhouse, other countries have established growth and investment strategies of their own, positioning themselves as what we call "emerging markets." As hard as it may be to believe, some still consider China to be one of those countries.

She Will Shake the World

One sign that has risen well beyond that came in 2018, when the largest stock market in the world, the onshore China market, announced it was opening to foreign investment. Despite its gargantuan size, the market had until then been closed to foreign investors. As such, no one in the United States had built a fund to invest in it. While international investors had bought Chinese securities via American Depositary Receipts (ADRs) or listings in Hong Kong (deemed "offshore"), the country's main stock market, its onshore one, had been closed off to outsiders.

I was managing portfolios at one of the world's largest emerging markets investment firms when the opportunity of a lifetime passed my way. A prospective client asked whether my team and I could build a fund that invests solely in the onshore China markets. Since I already had a successful history of pioneering investment funds in emerging markets, I readily agreed to investigate.

I longed to undertake the challenge of being among the earliest US investors in the Chinese onshore market, but the risks were not lost on me. I did not speak Mandarin, and China was a notoriously closed society. Further, the market was nascent and fraught with political, economic, and social hazards.

Plus, I was a quantitative investor. My process was built on objectivity. I used computerized systems to systematically evaluate a company's characteristics. Using technology, I could invest in hundreds of stocks at once, benefiting from breadth instead of depth. Could this arm's-length process work in the case of China, where the "invisible hand" of government plays such a significant role? By this point, I had visited China frequently enough to know that the Chinese economy was an enigma in more ways than one.

In the land of the Middle Kingdom, the visible dichotomies mirror its ideological ones. From my Western point of view, China is composed of tradition, transition, mystery, and questionable ruling methods, all in equal parts. It is a thriving capitalistic economy under communist party rule. Just a few years ago, it would have been hard to imagine the country as a consideration when devising an investment plan. But today, China co-leads the pack of world economic leadership.

For the capitalist financial system to work, a society needs people to generate money and to spend it. One of China's greatest assets, positioning it to earn the title of the world's second greatest economy, is people power. Populations of "small towns" in China boast numbers greater than the entire state of Mississippi.

Yet as China's economy emerges, it offers a striking juxtaposition in its quest for peace and prosperity. While the United States and China represent the largest economies in the world, the largest drivers of growth, and the largest polluters on earth, their pathways to get here have been markedly different.

China challenges our most basic Western notions. The country has achieved scale in secrecy, rocketed growth while maintaining stability, and grown a burgeoning middle class, yet remains rife with massive violations of human rights.

As the country's economy has risen, China has awakened from a great slumber of hundreds of years and, today, embodies the epitome of a rising power, potentially reentering another one of its great dynastic eras. Two hundred years ago, Napoleon Bonaparte recognized the potential within the country, warning us all: "Let China sleep, for when she wakes, she will shake the world."

Understanding China's dichotomies is more than an intellectual exercise. The paradoxes prompt us—today's investors, policy makers, and market participants—to ask several unsettling questions: Is China the next great market and a world power? Perhaps more profoundly, we know our investments do more than generate returns. They build tomorrow's ecosystem. Is China a sustainable ecosystem in which we want to invest and that we want to empower?

Hot Stocks in the Heart of Capital

As China's onshore market emerged, I couldn't resist the challenge. With the impressive breadth and depth in the local market and its vast mispricings, I could find copious opportunities for investment. In established, developed markets, "unicorn" stocks—those with attractive growth prospects, good management teams, and yet an underpriced valuation—were hard to find, but in China, the opportunities seemed almost ubiquitous.

I decided to go for it. I was going to launch the firm's onshore China A fund. But first my team needed to raise capital.

The day on which I was scheduled to do one of my first fundraisers was problematic. I awoke not in my hotel room but in an emergency room. I had some unusual pain the night before, and my doctor had recommended I visit the ER given the late hour.

By 6 a.m., I was becoming desperate. "Can I be discharged soon?" I asked the nurse. I would be speaking to some of the world's most sophisticated investors in just two hours' time.

She smiled at me—a calming, knowing smile of someone who had cared for many working mothers like me or who was one herself. "Let me get the doctor," she responded.

The tests confirmed that the baby I was carrying was safe. My daughter was due in six months, and we had a long road ahead before her arrival. But before her, I had to deliver this other baby—our firm's new China fund.

After I was discharged, I showered quickly back at my hotel. I then scurried down to the lobby level conference room, suited and booted, briefcase in hand, and slides on screen.

I began to describe the transformation that had occurred in China over the past two decades. I told my audience that when I visited Shanghai in 2004, on the bullet train to downtown, I had reflected then at the irony that this emerging powerhouse was the same country that hosted volunteers from my school just months earlier to help with hunger and poverty efforts. Out my window, the transformation had been clear: skyscrapers with futuristic architectural designs juxtaposed to the alleyways of old China. The view up ahead was high-rise, glass-filled, majestic buildings, but the alleyways were decrepit, old China, with broken windows, smoke-covered walls, peeling paint, overcrowded homes, and barred windows.

As I walked down the broad, fresh, beautifully manicured sidewalk in Shanghai, alongside the Yangtze River with a sea of cranes in the distance, I marveled at the city's beauty as well as its port. While I was no maritime expert, I watched the huge tanker ships and cargo carriers busily crowd and pass, load and upload. I knew it viscerally: *This was the busiest port in the world.*

Deng Xiaoping, China's 12-year leader credited with transforming the once languid nation into an industrial powerhouse by incorporating capitalist ideals, chose Shanghai as the North Star of the country's commercial dawning. "If China is a dragon," he said, "Shanghai is its head." Deng's vision became a bustling reality.

Today, Shanghai is marked by its colorful Bund, dressed with marquees that declare the Chinese people's love for their city, and crowned by the skyline's landmark pink pearl. It is one of the world's most populous cities. When Deng Xiaoping made his declaration decades ago, what is now the recognizable scene of downtown Shanghai was a few buildings on open land. Today, it's among the most electric, dynamic, cosmopolitan destinations. Of the 10 tallest buildings in the world, five of them stand in China. The Bund is home to the second tallest, at 2,073 feet—the Shanghai Tower.

How did China achieve this scale?

Through economic liberalization. The year 2020 marked the fortieth anniversary of Premier Deng Xiaoping's liberalization strategy. My college economics professor had elegantly described this approach as "opening up," to enable the export of goods and import of massive amounts of capital.

Since then China has provided a dramatic case study in how emerging markets can shift from their historic manufacturing base, with low-wage workers, to growth-oriented bases, which are less subject to macro cycles.

With its centrally planned system, in 2014 China embarked on a strategic imperative, dubbed "The New Economy," which aimed to shift the country's policy away from reliance on manufacturing toward one being powered by innovation.

Alongside the opening of its economy, China also opened its stock markets, where shares of public companies are traded. They technically opened the stock market in 2002, trying out a series of liberalization efforts, but each variation limited investors' ability to repatriate their capital. Any good CFA knows that above all, our first objective is preservation of capital. Regulators sought feedback from investors and adjusted.

In 2017, China launched an updated program, which finally abolished the repatriation restrictions. This was the milestone I had been waiting for. At this point, international financiers were able to invest—and I wanted to be early.

So I jumped at the opportunity when the client asked whether we could build a strategy to access this market. There was a lot to love. China is not only home to a powerhouse economy but also to a huge stock market. The local market has as many listed securities as the United States, approximately 3,500. The stock market is the most liquid in the world, making it cheap to trade stocks locally. Given the large consumer base and rapid technological progress, the stock market offers some of the largest and most creative companies, including the largest HVAC company in the world (Midea Group), the largest beverage company in the world (Kweichow Moutai), and innovative car companies that produce battery-powered vehicles, self-driving cars, and even flying-car technology.

Other aspects drew me in too. For one, the Chinese market doesn't move alongside that of the United States, given that the markets' respective investors are so different. As an example, in 2005, the correlations between the US market and China's were exactly zero. That's exciting from a risk-management perspective, as investors can smooth their risk exposure across lowly correlated investments.

There was more. China's stock market is rife with mispricings, which enables astute investors to find attractive buying opportunities. In the local market, trade ideas are often blasted out on WeChat chatrooms, and stocks typically trade far from their intrinsic value. This is a stock picker's dream. Chinese investors invest with a gambler's mentality. In fact, a study of trading patterns in Taiwan (which China considers to be its territory) revealed market liquidity was significantly higher on days when the lottery was closed. The culture is one that has become accustomed to gaining quick fortunes and doing what it takes to amass it, as proven by its influx of new money, the luxury skyscrapers built at warp speed, and the latest model luxury cars that light up the streets of metro areas at night.

Yet another advantage was that the market was opening. Never before had global investors been able to access the market, so there was only one direction for allocations to go: up. With flows of capital into the country, that would surely push up stock prices.

I was enthralled by the opportunity. Having long been invested in "frontier" market stocks, I saw China as having the pricing inefficiency of frontier markets with the scale of the United States. Yes, I was acutely aware of its dictator-based economy. As a dutiful quant, I reran the analysis and confirmed what I already knew: Stock markets of democratic countries perform in line with those of more autocratic countries. Uncomfortable as it is, I had come to accept that at a certain stage of development, a different political approach can make sense.

In summary, when it came to China, I was all in.

All Rules Are Off

I was hardly alone. The opportunity piqued other investors' interests, and the China onshore story became a dominant phenomenon, one of the hottest investment topics in 2018 and beyond. The secret was getting out, and I felt the urgency to act if I wanted to be early.

But some astute investors in the United States were concerned. These were experienced allocators, some of whom had actually tried investing in China before. They asked me, "How can we trust the local authorities? How can we even trust them to return our money when it's time?"

It's true. The judiciary system in China was opaque at best and corrupt and aligned with the state's whimsical interest at worst.

I relayed what I knew: It was in China's interest to align with international investors' standards. The Chinese would have much to lose if they were to violate our expectations.

Still, I needed to do more research. Liberalizing an economy is no small feat.

Given the governance and regulatory uncertainty, I was surprised when news agencies reported the potential inclusion of China's onshore market in established indices. It seemed very early and somewhat risky for a country with such governance questions to be included in mainstream allocation plans. My investors worried too. Telephones at my office in Boston rang busily and emails piled up.

As one of the largest emerging and frontier market investors, I had the classification agencies' ear as they conducted their analysis. I long admired the agencies' diligence of market dynamics and their insistence on established market norms. They worked closely with the country's governments and financial leaders to ensure adequate steps were being made. My friend Sebastien Lieblich ran classifications for many years at Morgan Stanley Capital International (MSCI), one of the leading emerging market benchmark providers.

At one of his stopovers in New England a while before, in a large group setting, I had asked him why he was always looking for upgrades. Pragmatically, for me, it's clear—these events create huge return events for my investors, and my fiduciary duty is to deliver these types of returns. But why for Sebastien?

He said that their group's primary objective is to offer the full investable universe to their clients. As his tall frame seemed to fill our fishbowl auditorium, his voice softened a bit when he explained that, in addition, it was a social good. Sebastien went on to explain why it was in the best interest of these economies to receive foreign capital to help push their economies forward. Investors likewise benefited from having a broader universe to pick from, so the process was a win-win.

Many other investors have watched countries such as Saudi Arabia change their market structures, even change their weekend schedule, to align with international standards. Painstakingly, a handful of countries went through these transitions, eschewing bureaucracy and decades of tradition, to meet the standards of institutional investors.

So, I had to give Sebastien a call when I heard the rumors that China would be included in the emerging markets index. I couldn't fathom why. Yes, repatriation restrictions had been removed, and yes, I agreed, that was critical. But what about the rest? There was no shorting market, and the settlement standards in China clearly misaligned with MSCI's checklist. Was the classification team in fact pushing China as they had pushed other countries before?

Within months, the answer was clear. MSCI announced it would be including the A-shares in its mainstream index, albeit at limited weight. No further changes would be required for the initial implementation. I, along with many members of the financial world, was astounded.

Not only had China not met the benchmark's stated requirements, but when China insisted on their own terms, the international investment community acquiesced.

Including the shares traded on China's onshore market[1] is one example of how fundamentally foreign investment transforms emerging markets' equity markets. In this case, if the catch-up strategy continues as it is, China could represent at least half of the mainstream emerging markets benchmarks. This raises the question of China's categorical standing: Are they a developed market, or have they now reached stand-alone market status? In light of China's transformation, should we rethink the concept of emerging markets altogether? Noting MSCI's willingness to shift its standards, how "standard" was that construct to begin with? China not only led the game, but it's fair to say they changed it. In the future, how many other emerging markets will reach this stature? What will happen to the West's rules then?

Trade War or Tech War

While the flow of capital was compelling, it was also anxiety-provoking to see China's power in resetting the rules. China's power in rule-setting was playing out on another stage as well: the development of twenty-first century infrastructure —technology.

To launch the China fund, I would need to show investors that the China opportunity could persist despite opposing power moves and political dynamics. I was asked to prove this fact in front of the red-hot eye of the press.

In 2018, I sat across the table from a *Forbes* reporter. I reiterated the strategy's investment process, which used a series of screens to identify good investment opportunities. The strategy's strength was breadth, not necessarily depth. I could cover the whole market with screens and objectively analyze these stocks while staying above the fray of getting into the minute details. I felt like I had sold the reporter on my vision for the opening of China's stock market and the power of a data-informed approach, but he still had questions.

"Tell me you don't own these stocks." He pointed at the tech companies listed on the front page of the day's journal.

"I've only been looking at them," I told him. He was referring to the day before, when Senator Marco Rubio had lambasted China's listings in the United States and insisted on blacklisting these securities. Frantic selling had ensued.

It had been a hard sell at work. We tended to trust our models and resist judgmental overrides, but we were in the middle of a trade war fought between two epic powers. Never before had my investments been so political.

"Political risk seldom impacts the economy," I relayed to the reporter, reaffirming my investment strategy. But was it credible? Political risk seldom impacts the economy, but, clearly, sometimes it does.

I was sweating. China's power and possibilities were endless, but the risk was real too.

I soon came to realize that there was more to the story. A politician of one country criticizing the politics of another should have been a tip-off. The trade war between the United States and China, one of the great struggles of the past decade, is in fact more of a tech war. China's investments in unparalleled high technology have stood at the heart of the contest. For example, the United States has consistently blacklisted Huawei, the third-largest smartphone company in the world (after Samsung and Apple). It claimed that Huawei posed a security risk and penalized it by reducing its access to key computer parts such as chip makers, which the United States is the largest producer of. China knows that to reduce its reliance on foreign technologies and enhance its competitiveness against the United States in the tech war, domestic technology is indispensable.

Furthermore, to win the trade—or tech—war, China has exported its technology to other parts of the world. This is evidenced by its One Belt One Road (OBOR) initiative, a reincarnation of the historic trade route known as the Silk Road. By 2012, China ranked third worldwide in outward foreign direct investment (OFDI). For a country that had close to zero OFDI in 2000, this was a monumental leap. China now has the highest investment in sub-Saharan Africa, and for China's tech companies the African continent is a wide-open field. For example, China, led by Huawei, is in a bid to take over Africa's telecom networks.

Nor does any other country exemplify more the investments, benefits, and ramifications of investing in technology than China. Since declaring technology innovation as a national strategic imperative in 2014, the country has funded thousands of high-tech incubators across the country, literally forming new brightly lit, shining, and modern megacities along the way. To put the investment in perspective: in 2016, the US government spent just $1 billion USD on unclassified artificial intelligence (AI) programs. The Chinese government, in contrast, committed $150 billion.

A few years ago, a plastic bag of chopped onions labeled as "Made in China" landed in my freezer. China had disrupted the global supply chain with its low-cost labor, strategic planning, and geopolitical maneuvering. Visiting China recently, I saw this digital evolution right before my eyes in a restaurant in Chengdu, when my waiter "Little Blue" said, "Nǐ hǎo" with the best human impersonation that a robot could. Three days later, when I dragged a friend to the restaurant to witness the digital-savvy waitress, I saw that "Little Blue" had been replaced with "Motowaiter." I was told that "Little Blue" was with the technicians to fix a bug. While tech may be stealing routine jobs, it is creating more technical jobs.

The short-term destruction of jobs creates a real advantage for China, with its quickly aging population and declining labor force. To make up for its shrinking workforce, China needs to increase labor productivity, and Chinese industries have turned to automation to fill their current shortages.

As a result, China today rivals the United States in many measures of innovation, including research and development (R&D) funding, publications in scientific journals, number of patents, securing venture capital, and producing unicorn companies. The country boasts near-universal use of mobile technology and the strongest Internet infrastructure on earth. Its citizens, despite only 15% of the globe's population, account for nearly half of worldwide e-commerce.

China's technology infrastructure benefited from its historical manufacturing advantage. In the 1980s, with a GDP per capita of only $150, it commenced Phase 1 of its economic development, which was to "open up" and leverage its only international advantage: low-cost human capital. Labor costs would surely increase with success, policy authorities knew, and the labor advantage would soon be exhausted. It was imperative to develop other advantages to avoid becoming trapped in this phase of development.

Phase 2 involved unabashed copying with a "do not fear" attitude toward copyright law. By learning and imitating from the products that the cheap labor produced, a pathway was carved to allow the country to obtain knowledge and technology—key growth factors for continued progress. As Fan Gang, director of China's National Economic Research Institute (NERI) once shared, "There is no shame in imitation! What is a developing country to do otherwise?"[2] As knowledge spills over, Phase 3 transitions toward innovation, which led us to China's competitive position today.

China was once an enabler of tech development led by the Western world, but today it is an innovator. This fact fuels both greed and fear. As investors, we're hungry. As global citizens, we wonder what will become of technology in the hands of autocratic leaders. What happens when that technology extends through the full One Belt One Road corridor that China has built? Will the United States be left behind?

Sino-Sustainability: How China Went Woke

While China's rise in technology has been eye-opening, its tremendous growth has created large problems as well. Ever since the Paris Accords on global warming were signed in 2015, China, like many other countries, has proclaimed what they will contribute. President Xi Jinpeng announced, for instance, the pursuit of "Beautiful China" to combat the pollution of air and rivers. Yet what is left unsaid is their need to quell social unrest due to fouled water and sun-blanketing smog.

China's limitations on its citizens' freedom have chilling outcomes.

While its technology has brought economic advancements, there is a downside as well. Reports show that there is now a camera watching every 20 people. Millions of girls are lost in China each year due to abortions and infanticides, an unfortunate consequence of the country's prior one-child policy and advanced medical technology.

Grisly stories abound, like the prominently posted *Wall Street Journal* article entitled, "The Nightmare of Human Organ Harvesting in China." The article explained that "prisoners of conscience—Falun Gong members, Uighur Muslims, Tibetan Buddhists and 'underground' Christians—have . . . had their organs forcibly removed."[3]

As investors begin to prioritize sustainability in their investments, how can we possibly justify that China should represent a meaningful portion of a sustainable asset-allocation strategy? In particular, how could I do it? I was running not only pioneer emerging market strategies, but I was also launching innovative sustainability solutions. Under my leadership, I was managing the first quantitative strategy to become a signatory of the United Nations' Principles for Responsible Investing. Stories like this headline made it increasingly difficult to justify China as a "responsible" investment.

I read about these human rights violations and immediately called a Chinese friend. Sheryl was a stock analyst, and I was hopeful she could offer a different perspective. Hearing my concerns, she told me, "Americans will never understand." Her comments were not helpful. They were reminiscent of the doublespeak that often surrounds China.

On a prior trip, I had visited a mosque in Xi'an. Dozens of worshippers gathered in the stone structure and offered their holy prayers. In disbelief I took photos because I had learned as a schoolgirl that religion did not exist in China. Yet I had learned by then that what you hear is not what you should believe.

I should not have been surprised by Sheryl's remarks. Months earlier, we had flown kites together in Beijing's gigantic Tiananmen Square. The sky was overcast, and the wind was just right for our kites to glide. As we were leaving, I said, "I can't believe this is where such a devastating event occurred." I hoped she could give me a new twist on the Tiananmen Square massacre story.

Her face became flushed as she recounted the story of how thousands of students had gathered there on that fateful day in 1989. "They came here to declare their love for art when they met their doom." *What?* I wondered. I had understood that the Chinese citizenry did not know or at least admit to the event. She promptly ended, "The students ultimately fled the country, going to far-flung Australia and Holland to study art."

Her story was markedly different from what I had learned from the news. The students had risen against China's autocratic governance and had gathered to fight for political freedom. Noting the strange twist of her story, I asked her if she believed that the country's media was censored.

"Of course, it is," she told me matter-of-factly. "It is in an attempt to protect us," she added.

The doublespeak of Chinese officials has only continued in the decades since. Examples abound in the ESG (Environmental, Social, Governance) space as well. In the years since China came to the table at the Climate Change Conference (COP26) to sign the consequential Paris Agreement, surprising the world with its commitment to reducing carbon emissions, the country's investments in coal have soared.

In the days just before its market liberalization, China suspended nearly 25% of the stocks in its stock market. Citing excess volatility, the regulators pleaded innocence, saying they were only trying to protect investors. Yet the officials aren't helping me if I can't sell my stock.

More disturbingly, my own company parent's CEO, Wang Jian, wound up dead, having mysteriously fallen 50 feet to his death. The event followed a "corruption crackdown" of dozens of other CEOs who untimely fell ill, disabled, or were found deceased from tragic accidents.

In making sense of China's governance, the autocracy can be regarded as a benevolent overseer or as an emboldened tyrant. Years ago, during his administration, President Xi extended his term from a two-term limit to a lifetime tenure. Changing the rules does not encourage investors. On the other hand, China has unquestionably done more to alleviate poverty than any other country. Since Deng Xiaoping commenced his liberalization strategy, nearly a billion Chinese citizens—an astonishing number, one-seventh of the world's population—have been lifted out of poverty.

At the beginning of the 2010s, the middle class made up less than 1/10 of urban households in China; a decade later, it accounted for more than half. Once, Chinese consumers dreamed of bicycles, wristwatches, and washing machines; today they are more likely to yearn for SUVs and trips to Thailand. Nearly half of all people living in cities are under 35. Most are treasured only-children with little to no memory of a time when their country was poor. In a 25-year span, income per person in China has increased 13-fold in real terms, whereas globally it has less than tripled.

At the same time, human rights violations threaten continued investor holdings. I crossed the Charles River on a mild spring day to talk with former US ambassador to the UN Samantha Powers at the Harvard Kennedy School. I shared my vision of China as a huge market, liberalizing rapidly, creating vast opportunity, and spreading its wealth. I'll never forget how she rolled her eyes and laughed. "Tell me," she rhetorically declared, "what role does China have on the UN Human

Rights Security Council?" Given their record in depriving citizens' rights and curtailing their freedoms, not only does their current position cover up their violations, but it also condones the practices of other countries. I asked her for her views on the future of China. Unequivocally, she anticipated that more Chinese assets could be banned in the West and elsewhere.

I appreciated her position: It was intelligent, wellfounded, and, most importantly, well accepted. The banning of an investment, where I might have had a holding, would render my investment worthless.

As the public and private sectors merge and our objectives increasingly align, what happens in the political sphere increasingly matters in the private one. I could see this tension with my Chinese investments. Systems-level finance was coming to life before my eyes.

As we come to recognize that all capital has an impact, investors are beginning to understand that investments not only generate returns, they also build pathways to promoting peace and prosperity. This is the mission of today's ill-defined sustainability movement. While ESG (environmental, social, and governance) investing has heterogeneous objectives, its ultimate goal is using capital to build a more habitable, dignified ecosystem for our planet's people. I often ponder if my Chinese investments are supporting the autocrat at the top or if it is directed to responsible businesses that are creating jobs and livelihoods.

While China is rapidly adopting ESG standards and local stock exchanges mandate them, evaluating its commitment to sustainability remains a dubious exercise. As global investors and policy makers further flesh out the market, how will China's social developments be interpreted? Is China a model of development or a model of social demise? History is typically written by the victor.

The Next Center of the Universe

Ultimately, I did it. I delivered my babies. In 2018, I launched one of the United States' first onshore China A funds (with meaningful risk controls in place), and months later I delivered a beautiful baby girl.

I decided to ask a different stock analyst, Vivian, for her take. She confidently entered my office, complementing her androgynous haircut with a fancy Chanel scarf. I asked for her thoughts on the equity markets, and I wanted to understand more about the "invisible hand" of China's leaders. "Can I pick stocks based on their fundamentals, or is political risk just too great?"

After a short pause, she relayed to me the Chinese Communist Party's (CCP's) objective for delivering peace and prosperity, and she explained that political interventions may sometimes occur, assuring me that, as a long-term investor, I would benefit.

I admired Vivian's tilt toward broader humanitarian goals, and I inquired about her views on sustainability. "How can egregious human rights violations occur while China is looking to ensure peace?" I asked her politely but firmly.

Vivian dutifully explained China's commitment to ESG investing, and she included mention of the novel data disclosure standards that were soon to be required by the local stock exchange.

I pushed further for additional color on regulation for company-level labor standards, carbon commitments, and enforcement of both.

Vivian deftly pivoted to explain to me that China has lifted nearly a billion out of poverty. She relayed, confidently, that Americans will never understand, but that goodwill toward the CCP is high.

We spoke further about China's outlook before I thanked Vivian for her views and shook her hand. She packed her bag in her leather purse and stood to brace the cold weather that awaited her.

I pushed the button for the elevator, which quickly arrived. Vivian walked in with a quick and graceful gait. As the doors closed, she smiled wryly at me and said in her proper British- and French-tinted accent, "Did you know that I am a member of the Communist Party?"

2

Gem on the Pacific Rim

Vietnam: From a War-Torn Past to a Sizzling Future

My stomach churned as the engine of my prop plane blasted my ears. I had been up much too late the night before, celebrating my good friend's wedding at a Thailand resort, and I was sneaking away for a couple days for a side trip to Angkor Wat. When we landed, I found the airport was tinier than that of my home airport in the rural South. I descended the rickety portable stairs and walked to the customs room to receive my visa. I listened to the chip-chomp of the mechanical stamps churning out visas to each passenger. When my turn came, I noticed suddenly that I was the last in line.

The passport agent looked with concern at my passport. He left to speak with his coworkers, and they gathered to discuss me in Khmer, a language I couldn't understand. Once the conversation ended, one of the guards approached me. He whispered, "There's a problem. You're traveling with a full passport which cannot be updated, it seems."

No way, I thought. *I'm a frequent traveler. I've never had trouble passing in and out of countries.* I was skeptical, but I played nice.

After a long pause, he continued. "I can help you," he said, "but you have to pay me. Ten dollars, in US currency."

I could tolerate that. It was a reasonable way out.

But he went on. "This is not allowed, you know. You can't tell any-one," he said. "If you do, I will get in trouble. And so will you. You will never be allowed to leave the country."

I handed him a $10 bill and proceeded to the exit. As I got into a taxi, I reflected: in Cambodia, a measly ten-spot will satisfy corrupt passport officials.

At least I was able to sleep in a spacious, well-appointed hotel room in Angkor Wat, loosely translated as "City of Temples." The next morn-ing, after a buffet breakfast, I walked, entranced, through its complex of Khmer structures—a Buddhist pilgrimage site for almost a thousand years. My tour guide, Tiro, was born in the late 1970s, just like me. He spoke fluent English and was eager to share the details about the temple.

When I asked him about Cambodia's recent history, though, Tiro lowered his voice. We sat in the grass as he spoke quietly about the Khmer Rouge regime. The notorious killing fields of his youth had al-tered his life decisively. Both of his parents had been killed in the Khmer Rouge genocide, along with 1.5 to 2 million other Cambodians, when he was still an infant. Tiro later lost his right arm by accidentally stepping on a still-active land mine—a scourge in this region, as in other parts of the world—one that was likely left behind after the 1978 invasion of Cambodia by the Vietnamese, who were seeking to remove Pol Pot, the notorious head of the Khmer Rouge.

The courses the two countries have taken since that time are mark-edly different. Having a centrally dictated economic plan is no guarantee that a country will prosper. Ravaged by war, Cambodia stands in stark contrast to its similarly razed neighbor. While Cambodia has no trade-able stock market today, Vietnam has risen as a darling of emerging and frontier market investors. Enthralled by Vietnam's emergence, I often re-flect on how Cambodia might have been able to take this alternative path. Vietnam is a shining example of the power of investment capital.

The Fall of Saigon

Several years prior to launching the China fund, my investment thesis on Vietnam turned positive. The stock market was broader than nearly any other in the frontier markets universe, and I could identify dozens of compelling investment opportunities. But Vietnam was notorious for dubious data, so I needed to confirm the prospects in person by visiting the country and speaking to the people.

I asked my husband Nikhil to join me, along with Jasper, our toddler son, and Griffen, who was still an infant. I was no stranger to balancing children with my career. When my boys joined these trips, Nikhil would come along as our family "manny." In the first year of our marriage, I had been offered the opportunity to run the world's first frontier markets equity fund. The role came with a condition to spend time abroad. Nikhil committed to me then that he would enable me to keep it up. Incredibly, and despite the burden of children, he followed through.

We landed a couple of days ahead of my meetings to travel as tourists. Our first stop was the Cu Chi Tunnels, in Ho Chi Minh City, where we trekked along an elaborate, muddy network of underground tunnels built by the Viet Cong, stretching 120 miles from the outskirts of Saigon to the Cambodian border. It was sobering to walk these tunnels, a powerful reminder of a world gone wrong. Tiny villages had been built underground so soldiers could be housed, along with transporting communications and supplies, as a base from which they could mount surprise attacks. A staggering 45,000 soldiers had died protecting these tunnels.

Afterward, during lunch, I started receiving frantic calls and emails from my office back home. A colleague emailed me: "URGENT: can you please respond ASAP?" Oil prices were dropping precipitously, and my largest client was contemplating a withdrawal. They worried that a drop in oil prices meant oil-exporting emerging market countries would take a hit.

I marveled at the irony of these urgent emails. While Vietnam was technically a net oil exporter, their economy was running full throttle, and they were consuming more and more refined oil to run their plants. I could see the energy bristling all around me. Back home, investors were panicking about falling oil prices, but here it seemed the people were rejoicing in the streets. Lower oil prices meant that they could manufacture more and run even faster. Clearly, Vietnam was no one-trick pony. The price of oil was yesterday's news.

And so was the war, for that matter. The tour guides were remarkably blasé about a war whose death rate was staggering: 1.1 million fighters from the North perished in the conflict, along with 250,000 South Vietnamese soldiers and over 58,000 Americans, plus two million civilians on both sides. Fifty years later, the war seemed like a distant dream. The tunnels are now a popular tourist destination. New Vietnam is roaring away from its past.

Dairy Queen: Innovation in the South Pacific

The next day, while my husband and kids were still jet-lagged and drowsy, I slipped out of our hotel to start my reconnaissance. The whizzing of the mopeds caught me off-guard. There seemed to be a 100:1 ratio of mopeds to automobiles. I laughed as I noticed at each red light, hundreds of moped drivers would line up in rows, as orderly as soldiers on parade; they would then roar off in unison when the light turned green. I decided I would go that way too.

With help from my bellman, I hailed an English-speaking *Xe Om* and hopped on the back of his moped. I had learned from prior travels that the best intelligence comes from taxi drivers. In this case, my tour guide would be my moped driver.

As the wind blew through my hair, I marveled at the city around me. Ho Chi Minh City (HCMC) is Vietnam's sexy, dynamic, and dazzling megacity. The sidewalks were packed with people, and lively music spilled out from restaurants, apartments, and car windows.

I peppered my driver as he darted along. "What's your name?" I asked. "Thuc."

"Were you born here?"

"No, I was born in the rural area. I came here to support my family, and I send money back."

"Are you married?"

"No."

I gazed around as he introduced me to HCMC's carefully planned districts. One district was for banking, another for arts, and still another for shopping.

As dusk started to fall, I asked Thuc to stop for a roadside treat. He spoke to the street seller, ordering a *cà phê sữa đá* iced coffee for himself and a *banh mi* sandwich for me. I was itching to try the iced coffee, but I've learned to avoid ice when I travel abroad. Still, the Vinamilk sticker on the stand caught my eye, and I asked Thuc, "Do you drink milk?"

He was confused by the question. I knew from my research back home that the Vietnamese were still developing a taste for dairy. He answered matter-of-factly, "Vietnamese people don't drink milk."

At another one of our stops, I marveled at this energetic maze, and I asked him, "Do you love living here?" He half-smiled at me and took off again.

When we stopped next, his eyes locked on mine in his tiny rearview mirror, and he said, "I'm ready for the revolution."

The uprising he was seeking had nothing to do with the rise of the proletariat. He wanted to take the leap into the middle class that so many Vietnamese were making.

Thuc pointed at the shops around us. Stores teemed with novel consumer goods: lotto tickets, SIM cards, ice creams, mixed in with Pandora jewelry and luxury tour packages. Thuc had achieved his original mission—stability, wealth, and hope—following a youth of near starvation after the protracted Vietnamese war. He was no longer hungry for basic needs but for success, esteem, and more.

Vietnam's youthful population and dynamism today stand in stark contrast to its past. The country has developed what so many emerging and frontier markets yearn for: a consumer-oriented economy. The consumer orientation relieves countries from the notorious dependency on commodity prices and protects them from global boom-bust cycles. In a domestic demand-driven economy, sovereign and corporate leaders can be more effective at managing their financial affairs.

Vietnam's proportion of young to old people has been a boon to its transition. The country is the fifteenth-largest globally by population, and its median age is only 30. Rapid urbanization has spurred a rapidly growing middle class that is well educated and able to spend. The country's literacy rates have soared during recent years to 93%. This middle-income group represents nearly one-third of its population, and private consumption accounts for 55% of Vietnam's GDP.

History still retains its hold on this population. Given the historical presence of the French and the Americans, many members of this youthful demographic speak French or English as a second language. And because the Vietnamese language is written in Latin script, rather than a character-based one as in other Asian countries, its citizens can access Western languages with relative ease.

That is not to say that the economic revolution has affected the political sphere in the slightest. Like China, Vietnam has benefited from a centrally planned economy. In December 1986, at the Sixth National Congress of the Communist Party of Vietnam (CPV), reformists led by Nguyễn Văn Linh, the party's then-new general secretary, implemented a series of free-market reforms known as Đổi Mới ("Renovation"). The goal was to transition the nation from a planned economy to a "socialist-oriented market economy." Private ownership of farms and factories was encouraged, economic deregulation instituted, and foreign investment welcomed.

In the 1990s, a time of manufacturing-based economies and vast globalization, the Vietnamese government lured global corporations by offering significant tax breaks, ready access to ports, and a population of young and highly literate workers willing to work for low wages. Given these enticements, globalization rolled in. Before long, Vietnam was experiencing a manufacturing boom. More than half the companies listed in the Fortune 100 had a presence in Vietnam. This country, while politically communist, had become a capitalist haven.

The capital infusions transformed lives and transformed the country's future. As foreign capital poured in, consumer sentiment scaled sky high, and luxury home values skyrocketed. Despite a quickly managed banking crisis, the country urbanized as Thuc, my moped driver, and others flocked to the cities. Vietnam attained "middle-income" status by the World Bank by 2013. By 2019, the United Nations ranked Vietnam as having "high human development" on the basis of its education, life expectancy, and per capita income; Vietnam had achieved among the highest HDI (Human Development Index) growth rates in the world.[1]

The moped stop for iced coffee provides one case example, among many others, of this transition. The United Enterprises of Milk Coffee Cookies and Candies was formed in 1978, and the company was rebranded as the Vietnam Dairy Company in 1993. Partly owned by the government, the company's motto, variously translated as "Make Vietnamese Taller" and "Stand Tall Vietnam," alludes to the belief that milk would help the population's physical stature.

In 2006, the company was publicly listed on the Ho Chi Minh Stock Exchange as the Vietnam Dairy Products Joint Stock Company (Vinamilk), and it has been one of the strongest stock performers over the past decade. Given that the Vietnamese population traditionally had little appetite for dairy—many Asians consider yogurt and other products made from lactating cows to be repugnant—Vinamilk's success wasn't assured.

The company's CEO, Mai Kieu Lien, known to many as "The Dairy Queen," ably steered the company from being a small, state-run firm to one of the country's most profitable brands. Now in her 60s, Lien is a vibrant woman who radiates the energy of today's HCMC and understands the power of Vietnam's consumer class.

In 2017, she shared, "Vietnam's rapid urbanization and rising incomes have led to a growing adoption of a Western lifestyle. This has led to a boom in fast-moving consumer goods such as dairy and beer. With Vietnam's population growing by a million every year, the potential consumer segment is a great opportunity, and the penetration rate for beer and milk products has not yet maximized."[2]

By then Lien had done much to reach this consumer segment, modernizing the company in the process. In 2014, Vinamilk built one of the most cutting-edge dairy factories in the world, one controlled by robots, a fact I found rather startling, given the abundance of low-skilled labor in Vietnam. By 2016, the company was supplying a national school milk program. Four years later it had a dominant 42% market share in the dairy category.

Today, Lien is recognized as one of Asia's most powerful businesswomen, having transformed Vinamilk "into one of Vietnam's most profitable brands but also a respected name across Asia."[3]

Investors are thirsty for exposure to Vietnam, with its large population of ambitious, hard-working youth. Vinamilk encapsulates the power of capital in creating new categories, and transforming economies, livelihoods, and people themselves.

Turbulence

This thirst for Vietnam shows in the pricing of the country's stocks. Although Vietnam is technically still a frontier market, it boasts the liquidity of many emerging markets today.

Investors can't get enough. Vietnam's hottest stocks often trade at their foreign ownership limit; investors must fight among themselves for these limited shares, and only the highest bidders can win.

That was a huge concern for my portfolio. I was enthralled by Vietnam's domestic growth, but it was all for naught if I couldn't invest. The companies' tight limits on how much foreigners could own meant that nearly all the attractive companies were trading at that limit. Vietnam's limits were far tighter than any other market, and I wanted to know if these might be relaxed.

I wasn't the only one. Other investors on my tour were similarly frustrated. Many of them participated in IPOs (initial public offerings). Vietnam was compelling, in part because of her massive privatization program and the opportunity to participate in the economy's local development. But as much as the government talked about these programs, foreign investors weren't getting access. The information wasn't shared broadly enough, and it wasn't shared clearly.

A consortium of other investors and I had set up a series of meetings with local market leaders in Hanoi for the next day, so my family and I had to get there.

My family and I arrived at HCMC's Tan Son Nhat Airport's domestic terminal for our flight up to Hanoi. The terminal was packed with people, every one of whom seemed to be in motion, darting to or from a plane. As an investor, I knew that the travel sector in Vietnam was booming. Seeing it played out in frantic dimensions brought that fact home.

Airlines were heavily discounted, and we had several flights to select from. We opted for VietStar since the cost to travel on this carrier was 75% less—a substantial savings for a family of four—than it would have been on VietAir, the recently privatized national airline.

As we checked in for our flight, I nervously noted that three other planes would be taking this same route at the same time. Then, as now, the HCMC–Hanoi route was the busiest one in Southeast Asia. *Is there enough airspace for all these flights?* The thought crossed my mind. *Will we bump each other out of the sky?*

We boarded a musty, creaky, decidedly vintage Soviet-built plane. We took our seats in the minuscule seats with limited legroom. Our fellow passengers—mainly Vietnamese families—shrugged off the usual safety precautions. The clicking of seatbelts being unbuckled sounded out almost as soon as our plane took off. From that point on, the aisles of the plane filled with wandering passengers, chatting and laughing, seemingly utterly relaxed, even as the flight continued upward at a 45° angle. While my husband and I clutched our tiny armrests in fear, Jasper grinned with excitement, and the rocking put Griffen right to sleep. Two hours later, we disembarked at Noi Bai Domestic Airport with relief. The passage, like so much else in Vietnam was rocky, but the outcome was good.

As an investor who always tries to stay a step ahead, I was well aware of present trends. The following year, the Trans Pacific Partnership (TPP) was on course to becoming the largest free trade agreement in history, covering 40% of the global economy. The agreement addressed such issues as tariffs on goods and services, labor and environmental standards, and issues of intellectual property.

Although TPP is commonly credited to the Obama administration, its origins actually date back to the presidency of George W. Bush who, in 2008, began talks with a group of four Pacific Rim countries that had entered into a trade agreement several years before. An expanded version of this agreement ultimately became the centerpiece of TPP, which was part of President Barack Obama's strategic pivot toward Asia.

In 2016, TPP was signed by 12 Pacific Rim countries—Japan, Australia, Peru, Malaysia, Vietnam, New Zealand, Chile, Singapore, Canada, Mexico, Brunei Darussalam, and the United States.

For its supporters, TPP promised to expand US trade and investment abroad, spur economic growth, lower consumer prices, and create new jobs, while also advancing US strategic interests in the Asia–Pacific region. Its detractors, who included US presidential candidates Donald Trump and Hillary Clinton, and others across the political spectrum, saw it otherwise. They were convinced that it would accelerate the loss of US manufacturing jobs, lower wages, and increase inequality.

On January 23, 2017, just three days after being sworn into office as president, Donald J. Trump signed an executive order pulling the United States out of TPP. Of all of TPP's signatories, Vietnam, with its large manufacturing base, had the most to gain from the agreement. Logically, then, it might have had the most to lose. When news of TPP's demise came out, many investors held their collective breath, waiting for the market meltdown that would follow.

The crash never happened.

The many experienced, long-time investors, both local and foreign, simply continued to invest. And Vietnam continued to thrive. To this day, it remains one of the world's strongest investment opportunities.

Vietnam's ability to stay aloft, even as TPP fell apart around it, came about for solid reasons. Trade and global flows powered the Vietnamese economy. Over the past several years, Vietnam had demonstrated to the globe its vast productivity and global contributions, enabled by capital injections. If the United States chose not to participate, surely others would step in. Other FTAs, such as the EU–Vietnam Free Trade Agreement, were in place, and Vietnam was positioned to attract foreign direct investment (FDI) without TPP.

Two years later, the remaining 11 nations from the TPP agreement enacted a new trade agreement called the Comprehensive and Progressive

Agreement for Trans-Pacific Partnership. The free trade of capital among
the remaining countries would keep this thriving economy aloft.

But its underlying base was even more wide-ranging than that. Vietnam had already successfully made the transition to a stable economy.
Its domestic reforms had centered on deregulation, trade liberalization,
and investment in human and physical capital. The country's liquidity
provided it with ballast. Its economy, by then, was fundamentally sound.

The Silver-Tongued Minister

Hanoi was not Ho Chi Minh City. Here, Vietnam's national flag—bright
red, with a yellow star at the center—flew ubiquitously from high on the
rows of flagpoles lining the sidewalks to cables stretched from one side
of a road to the other, like laundry on a clothesline. The city felt formal
and slow paced. The passersby could be described as elegant. Some wore
military uniforms; others wore fashionable clothes. The streets had an
out-of-time feeling, reminding me of those rainy days in Paris when the
past seems to come alive.

Hanoi was reserved compared to HCMC's dynamism, and the skies
were grayer on this particular day. Yet the first official meeting for foreign investors was staged in an impressive setting. Located in the Ba
Dinh District, the Ministry of Planning and Investment is housed in a
no-nonsense rectilinear building softened by a gracefully curving façade.
As I passed through its stately, ornate lobby, with golden columns and
reliefs, I couldn't help reflecting on the dramatic shift in fortunes of this
country, so recently impoverished and now one of the fastest-growing
economies on earth.

Entering the meeting room was like stepping into the burst of a
golden-tinted rainbow. The walls were chartreuse. At the center of its far
wall, Vietnam's flag was set against a vast mural featuring lotuses—the
country's national flower—in shades of lavender. Within this arresting setting Deputy Minister Dang Huy Dong sat peacefully on his throne-like
chair upon a stage to speak with us. We were served tea in bone china
cups and plates with golden rims.

With impeccable English, Dong introduced himself with silver-
tongued eloquence. (I later learned that his earliest jobs had been as
a translator.) With his prepared comments, he shared Vietnam's significant strengths. He spoke first of its well-educated, young, and sizable

workforce. Then he pointed out that it has one of the longest coastlines among Asian countries. Additionally, it benefits from the sociopolitical stability afforded by the communist system. This allows the country to set a long-term vision and execute it. For example, through tax credits and friendly competition among Vietnam's states, the country strategically drew FDI from around the world.

His vision aligned with my experience. FDI in the country was robust, indeed, with commitments likely to hit US$20 billion that year.

Dong spoke at length of the strength of the country's manufacturing center. He explained in intricate detail the agreements that had been made with Korea and Japan to develop their technologies, largely as components for cell phones, and in return Vietnam received discounted loans for infrastructure development at home.

He anticipated the questions from his audience, many of whom were frustrated with the botched IPO processes, the pace of privatizations, the restrictions in putting capital to work, and the lack of clarity. He assured us of transparency as he described the nodes of government that are involved and the processes entailed. He implored us to recognize that while one or two IPOs may have generated adverse news coverage, Vietnam sets the pace in privatizations with hundreds of events each year. Foreign ownership limits, which constrained my strategy, would be relaxed in due course, he assured our group, deftly anticipating my question.

Dong concluded his optimistic comments by confidently predicting that future trade agreements with Europe, Russia, and Korea would open his country's markets up further, with exports fueling growth and buttressing external accounts.

His comments reminded me that the flow of capital to Vietnam not only shifted the arc of its history up to the present, it also has enabled the country to shift to the future, which will feature less globalized manufacturing and more technology prowess. It is worth adding some perspective here. Whereas China's tech sector has long been a driving force in its economy, Vietnam belongs more in the stage of future promise.

With high-speed growth, Vietnam's digital economy is the next dragon being unleashed. The country has been displacing China in global supply chains for the past 10 years. In fact, China imports many of its raw technology materials, including the majority of iPhone components, from Vietnam. Far more important to its economy, producing Samsung smartphones and spare parts forms the majority of

Vietnam's exports. As recently as 2020, a full 28% of its GDP was tied directly to Samsung's economic health. With investments in Vietnam totaling $17 billion, Samsung was then the country's largest single foreign investor.[4]

Vietnam is not only a manufacturer of global technologies, but a rapidly growing user as well. According to the behemoth Singapore sovereign fund, Temsaek, "Southeast Asians are the most engaged mobile internet users in the world . . . . There are 360 million internet users in the region, and 90% of them connect to the internet primarily through their mobile phones."[5]

Effectively, the country sits today at the beating heart of the tech and telecom revolution.

Environmental and Social Risks at the Red River Delta

You can always count on a government official to provide a glowing report. Yet I make these trips to investigate what can't be read from the headlines back home. Following the meeting with the minister, I met with a small group of investors at a French café. One of them brought along a friend, a blogger-journalist who once lived in Washington, DC, but had returned to his home city.

Our conversation quickly centered on him. He spoke to us quietly, looking alternatingly over his shoulder and then past our heads to his front. He told us he needed to be careful what he shared. He feared that someone could be listening, for journalists could be arrested if they deviated from the state's messaging. At all times he had to be careful about whether he was being followed. He warned that "facts" I would hear during this heavily controlled investor trip might be canned, and he asked me about the line about country growth that I had heard several times. "They may be from different sources," he relayed, "but are they relayed in the exact same phrases?"

He had a point. I glanced at my phone as he spoke, googling for details about corruption in Vietnam. One site covered corruption and limits on journalistic freedoms. According to Vietnam's 2016 Press Law, journalism exists to serve as the voice of the Communist Party and state. Censorship is in full force. In view of this, Vietnam is ranked at number seven, just above China, on the Committee to Protect Journalists' list of the 10 most censored countries.

Perhaps he had a coffee too many, but his jitters put me on high alert. Abruptly, the man said goodbye. When I looked up, he was already gone.

Although the journalist was speaking of government suppression, it reminded me of another source of instability. The sequence of events in the summer of 2014 cast a pall on the future. Until that time Vietnam had been a strong investment. Quarter after quarter, the market went in only one happy direction. Yet in May that year an incident occurred off the coast of Vietnam, just south of the Chinese border. I received a text message from a broker one evening with a video attachment. I clicked the play button and watched as a huge, towering Chinese ship steamed after two small Vietnamese fishing boats. The large vessel then collided with one of the boats, which capsized. CNBC called the incident "the most serious deterioration of relations . . . since Vietnam's invasion of Cambodia."[6]

The story was more than David versus Goliath; at root was the matter of disputed sovereign territory. China claimed the sea, while Vietnam insisted she was the rightful owner. Nobody was killed in the incident, but the event incited a furor, resulting in anti-Chinese riots in Vietnam, the death of multiple protestors, and a dramatic fall in the stock market. While a series of tiffs ensued, the market stabilized by the end of the summer. Still, I was acutely aware that continued disputes could present a shock to my portfolio.

That's why I decided to follow up with Vietnam's largest drilling company. Few understood more about the offshore dynamics than the management team of PetroVietnam Drilling & Well Services, with operations from the Red River Delta all the way south. While on the ground, I took the opportunity to meet with the company. I was ushered into their offices alongside a few other investors. We sat at a high-gloss, veneered table, and when the management team entered a few minutes after, I was startled to find it was entirely comprised of women. I had worked in oil and gas for years as an investment banker at Goldman Sachs; this was the first time I met a majority female management team in the industry.

The company's CFO, Ho Ngoc Yen Phuong, firmly took command of the meeting. She stood before us with her small frame showing determined confidence and her voice stern and clear. She talked us through the latest financial results, explaining where the company had exceeded expectations and where they faltered.

When she invited questions, I was the first to raise my hand. I asked the burning question on my mind: "Could you please share your views on the company's risks as presented by China, especially given the recent skirmishes in the South China Sea?"

Her round eyes bore squarely into mine. "The East Seas," she corrected me firmly. Her answer said everything I needed to know. The meeting ended shortly thereafter.

While Vietnam's domestic sociopolitical risk seemed low, the risk of a geopolitical dispute remained. That mattered a lot. The past decade has been rich with major geopolitical disputes that have sent markets crashing, returns tumbling, and wiping out investors. In Vietnam's case, one of its greatest strengths—that extended coastline and its rich offshore reserves—was also one of its greatest risks. The country remains susceptible to strife along this vast stretch.

Another great risk to Vietnam's coastline is the threat of climate change. Since the coast is densely populated, Vietnam is among the earth's most vulnerable countries to rising sea levels and more frequent typhoons, droughts, and landslides. I was startled a decade ago when an economic officer at the US Consulate spoke openly about his concerns of the rising waters in the Red River Delta. This terracotta-hued region lies at the heart of northern Vietnam, and it is home to one-third of the country's population, producing its most critical products—rice, fisheries, and, increasingly, technology. Samsung and other companies have poured billions into the region.

The consul spoke openly with me about the value at risk of this rich, fertile land. "The economic consequences could be significant," he shared, "as Vietnam's key assets are located in precisely the most vulnerable regions: the low-lying coastal regions and the river deltas." What a contrast that was. Just the day before, the Minister of Planning had boasted about the country's manufacturing facilities on the coastline. Vietnam's other great industry, agriculture, accounts for two-thirds of the country's employment and roughly one-third of exports.

Economic distress could indirectly cause social unrest, but the social consequences could likely be more direct. Crop failures, caused by adverse weather events, had the potential to cause poverty, malnutrition, and food security imbalances in nearly 20% of the population, reversing the remarkable progress of recent years. The consequences would be particularly felt by poorer communities and laborers. The country's president, Nguyễn Xuân Phúc, spoke of the wider ramifications when he explained that the "devastating consequences may well erupt into geopolitical tension and instability, damaging peace, security, development and prosperity."[7]

The dynamic Red River Delta epitomizes how capital has transformed a region from untouched forest to vibrant opportunities. Yet it also showcases the risks that must be considered. Having achieved its economic objectives, how Vietnam manages its risks, corruption, climate, and China likely foretells its future.

His Eyes Are Always Watching

After the week in Vietnam, I felt that my visit was successful. The ethos and vitality of the people I met validated the data showing a favorable emerging market environment, although I had an understanding of the risks to my thesis. The journalist's whispered words haunted my thoughts, but once I tuned the model to account for corruption and related risks, Vietnam was irresistible. Ultimately, I would invest, but over time, I'd shift exposures more toward Vietnam's thriving consumer sector.

On the last day of our journey, Nikhil, the kids, and I still had a full day of exploration available to us. The tourism industry was clearly thriving, and we had plenty of options. First, we descended the stairs to our hotel's underground bunker, where Jane Fonda and Joan Baez had once hidden as American bombs rained down on them.

Griffen became scared, and we headed for sunlight after that. Nikhil and I took our trusty double stroller for a long walk to the Ho Chi Minh Mausoleum, the final resting place of the country's revered communist leader.

As we walked along, a giant billboard of "Uncle Ho's" face on a street post caught my eye. In the stylized image, the leader was holding a young baby. I stopped for a moment to snap a photo of my own baby beside the poster. As I put my camera away, I mused that the intent of the poster was surely to extend the leader's legacy through another generation.

At the mausoleum, we lined up among the throngs of tourists. The line moved in an orderly fashion, and after some time, we entered a long, dark hall, walking in a single file. A guide directed the crowd to form a circle. A bright spotlight shone on the old man's embalmed body.

"Are you sure he's dead?" Jasper reached up to me to whisper. He peered at the dead man in a stiff black suit, starched white shirt, and very lifelike face.

"Yes, I'm sure he's dead," I answered.

"Can he see us?" Jasper asked.

I thought about it. Maybe, just maybe, somehow he could still see us. Maybe, as the journalist had warned and the poster had suggested, his eyes would always be watching.

3

Global Flows

Spotlight on Saudi Arabia: The Greatest Story That Nobody Knows

I was already acquainted with the Middle East when I visited Saudi Arabia in 2011. Having spent time in such neighboring Gulf states as the United Arab Emirates (UAE) and Kuwait, I was familiar with the region's desert heat, Bedouin culture, and extraordinary history, which took such a radical turn after the discovery of oil in the 1930s.

This time I'd traveled 6,000 miles from my home in New England on a hunch—the same impulse that fuels investors all around the world. If my instincts were correct, I was about to uncover the investment story of my life.

Arriving in the Gulf this time felt like traveling to the future—at least at first. My first stop was the glitzy, hypermodern city of Dubai—a mecca of glamorous, fast-moving, international sophistication. On this visit I discovered another, less glitzy side to this UAE city, one with scent-filled souks, where you can shop for spices and gold and sample the delicious cuisine served up by Indian expats at the local *dhabas*, road-side restaurants—as popular in Dubai as on the Indian subcontinent. In that part of town I glimpsed the city's squalor, too, the underbelly few tourists choose to see.

Then we headed on to Abu Dhabi—the UAE's capital—not as dynamic as Dubai but still oozing with wealth. I'd also spent time in slow-paced Kuwait, once the site of ancient trade routes leading from the Gulf into modern-day Syria.

So I felt I knew the real Middle East. That is, until I arrived in Saudi Arabia. Nothing prepared me to travel back in time the way I did from the moment I set foot on Riyadh's dusty ground.

I'd been noting the rise of the Gulf markets for some time. In particular, Saudi Arabia, which now has the largest economy and stock market in the Middle East. I was convinced that this vast desert country, poised between the Persian Gulf and the Red Sea, might soon emerge.

In 2010, the UAE and Qatar had started opening up, and Saudi Arabia—the most populous country in the region—was showing signs of economic development and market liberalization. Banks were expanding; real estate was being built. There were even indicators that the Saudi national ban on mortgages, which run counter to Islamic strictures against charging interest, was beginning to loosen.

Soon I started hearing rumors that the Saudi government was considering liberalizing its market—huge news in the investment world. As the UAE and Qatar had recently met established institutional standards, they were shoo-ins to be classified as "emerging markets" by major benchmarks, but the classification agencies were waffling. What was slowing them down? I suspected that the hesitation had to do with some development in Saudi Arabia—perhaps the agencies were considering doing all the inclusions in unison. Perhaps Saudi was negotiating for a deal so that it wouldn't lag behind its smaller neighbors. The data looked promising, and I sensed an impending upgrade.

Frustrated by the scarcity of solid, up-to-date research, I resolved to travel to Saudi Arabia to explore it from an investment perspective. I wanted to witness its transformation firsthand—hear it with my own ears, see it with my own eyes. I wanted to take a front row seat to this process to better understand its many nuances and permutations.

■ ■ ■

Visiting the country was a struggle from the first. Happily, one fight—the one to enter the country in the first place—was avoided. As my investment broker explained, my entry visa had likely been approved only because my husband would be accompanying me to the Gulf. A travel buff, he couldn't resist the trip. He would also serve as "the manny," caring for our infant son while I was in meetings.

Arriving in the Kingdom was a shock. In spite of its grand-seeming name, the King Khalid International Airport was primitive, a relic from a bygone age. The word *international* was more aspirational than anything else. (That word, though, becomes relevant once a year, when millions of Muslims arrive from all over the world to perform religious rites at the annual *haj*.) No one at the airport seemed to speak English at all, a situation that, with the exception of China, I'd never experienced in all of my travels. Arguments over paperwork had me shuttling from one floor in the airport to another as I negotiated Saudi bureaucracy, with its antiquated paper-based systems.

The place felt even more backward when I entered the ladies' room and encountered a distinctly retro sight—a squat toilet, the kind that consists of just a pair of footrests and a hole in the floor. As I would soon discover, to my horror, these were commonplace in Riyadh.

We arrived at night and walked outside to a desert sky clear and bright with stars, the weather warm and dry. We cruised in a white taxi down King Fahd Road, a highway in all but name, lined on both sides by blocks of anonymous-looking commercial buildings. In the distance, the Riyadh skyline looked underwhelming—nothing like what it would soon become.

Beyond the main thoroughfares, the city seemed eerily empty. Some of the streets that intersected with the main road were shabby. Yet even the humblest two-story strip mall, with its stone façade and painted signs in Arabic script, seemed exotic to me, so different from the ones I saw back home.

The next morning, eager to explore the city, we set out on an early walk, before the heat set in. Life on city streets was strict. Women weren't allowed to walk without a male escort. As the day wore on, it became swelteringly hot—about 120 degrees—and everyone disappeared, many taking refuge in the city's ubiquitous air-conditioned malls.

From a distance, all Saudi women looked alike, dressed as they were in *abayas*, sheet-like garments, usually black, that cover every inch of the body from the neck down, leaving just their hands exposed. All women—even tourists, such as myself—had to wear them wherever they went. As surprising as it may seem to us in the West, some Saudi women report feeling a kind of freedom in being covered. Some are said to dress stylishly, even provocatively, beneath their abayas. A certain amount of contraband, including forbidden bottles of alcohol, is said to be transported in the folds of these garments.

For me, wearing an abaya was nothing short of repressive. I was embarrassed each time I put mine on. Not being used to it, I tied it awkwardly above my head. I was sure that everyone passing in the street looked at me pityingly as a result. I was also scared of possible abaya-related trouble. If it slipped, revealing even just a sliver of flesh, you could be scolded, or even fined, by one of the religious policemen who were once ubiquitous in the city's streets.

One day, as I sat with my husband and son over lunch in the mall adjoining our hotel, a group of men dressed in the long white tunics, known as *thawbs*, suddenly appeared and surrounded our table. The religious police! They didn't speak but stood in silence, staring at me with daggers in their eyes. I was terrified. I soon realized that we must be sitting in the restaurant's men's section rather than in the family one, though the sections were unmarked. We scuttled away to the right area.

That incident summed up Saudi life for me. The strict austerity was maintained by what is left unsaid. No words, no signs. It is a frightening way to live. Yet even as these repressive incidents added up on my visit, I believed that modernity was on its way to the Saudi Kingdom.

The Commodities Rut

The story of Saudi Arabia's economic liberalization illustrates how radically emerging markets have transformed over the past 10 years. Alongside the dramatic growth of China, I consider the rise of the Gulf markets—and the Saudi one in particular—the most important investment story of the past decade. Its rapid embrace of foreign investment propelled the country from its Bedouin past and from its commodities-based economy to the next era in its development.

Saudi Arabia's geopolitical prowess is a result of remarkably recent history. For hundreds of years it was a land of desert-dwelling Bedouin peoples. The harvesting of date palms, its historic and religious sites, and its trading hubs for camel-carrying caravans, such as the ancient oasis of Hofuf, near the coast of the Persian Gulf, drove its economy. In 1933, two Americans were granted the exclusive right to prospect this region for oil. Over five years, their entourage grew to hundreds of people, and well #7 in Dhahran produced oil in 1938. The first tanker of commercial oil was dispatched in 1939, setting in motion its transition to rapid affluence.

Within decades, Saudi's abundant and low-lying pools of oil rocketed the country onto the world stage. As the government took control over local fields, the nation rose to geopolitical prominence, setting the price of the globe's most powerful commodity, oil. Nations thrived or died by this price, and the Saudis, with more oil capacity than any other, wielded immense influence at OPEC, the intergovernmental "cartel" that ensures adequate access to the fuel that has made the world move for nearly a century. Saudi's state-owned company, Saudi Aramco, became the largest and most profitable company in the world, even today.

One result of the region's cheap, abundant oil is palpable. The world's largest mosque is outdoors, hosting hundreds of guests six times a day—in a fully air-conditioned space. Despite visiting in the 100° heat, wearing the obligatory black abaya and carrying a toddler on my hip, I managed to keep cool.

But my first trip to the region was weighed down with skepticism. On landing in Dubai, it was impossible to miss the scrappy, home-printed signs that were literally Scotch-taped to airport posts. The signs read in capital letters: "WE KNOW OUR OIL WON'T LAST FOREVER. WE MUST DIVERSIFY." I chuckled at such activism. Out of curiosity, I visited one of the UAE's emerging prototypical cities, a "city of the future" called Masdar that develops and invests in renewable energy projects. The buildings were an early-stage, ham-handed attempt at evoking Stanford's technology hub but in the middle of a desert.

Back in Riyadh, the tone was muted. Speaking of the rise of renewables would be laughable and embarrassing if not insulting, so I was left puzzled. Why was Saudi contemplating an initial public offering (IPO) of its prize jewel, Saudi Aramco? With the ease at which the country could subjugate its people, why share the wealth? Had the Kingdom taken note of the waves of change toward a lower-carbon economy? Oil prices were falling, Saudi's oil reserves (immense as they were) were dwindling, and while the country's reserves remained robust, foreign capital would provide a cushion. Separately, while the Bedouin past still lingered in the subordination of women and lethargic work culture of smoke-pray-repeat, the Saudis had improbable visions of becoming a bastion of innovation. A decade-plus project called NEOM was introduced, aiming to "incubate and commercialize groundbreaking technologies to accelerate human progress." Could the Saudis be considering diversification for real? At scale?

The willingness to open up their economy is not universal among commodity-dependent emerging market countries. Many are too crooked to invest in and hence are not labeled either emerging or frontier. Examples include Iraq and Venezuela, both countries that lack institutions in place to safeguard institutional capital—or people. In major exporting countries with thriving stock exchanges, commodity dependency tends to align with corruption, civil unrest, and autocracy, as can be seen in countries like Russia and Nigeria. Saudi Arabia is often cited as the example that proves the rule, with its grotesque violations of human rights, lack of an independent judiciary, and extremist ideology.

The benefits of pulling off a transition from a commodity-dependent economy to a diversified one are immense. For one, oil dependency means the economic strength of the country is inherently tied to the boom-bust cycles of oil. Despite its century of dominance, oil remains the most volatile commodity in the world—even more so than bitcoin.[1] Over the last decade, investors and global leaders have been facing the coming reality of "peak oil," after which the demand for oil will lessen. While for decades the emergence of the developing world has led to excess demand for fuel to power up their economies, economists and investors alike are noting the opportunities that structural change would produce.

Additionally, oil demand is waning, as reasonable transport alternatives are increasingly available today, including biofuels[2] and carbon-free vehicles. In fact, the emerging markets are leapfrogging their adoption, as these substitutes are gaining disproportionate share. As examples, more than 90% of vehicles in Brazil are already using ethanol or sugar-based fuel,[3] and more plug-in vehicles are sold in China than in any other country.[4] The economic rationale to diversify is not limited to the downside of the long-term waning price of oil. There's an upside as well. The Gulf Cooperation Council (GCC) region has an inherent geographic advantage, located between wealthy Europe and rising Asia. The UAE is a case example on how to take advantage of this strategic asset. Over the past two decades, the UAE has developed a broad economic footprint, expanding beyond oil toward financial services and tourism. Today, Dubai's airport is the busiest one across the globe, contributing to 40% of the country's GDP and 10% of the nation's jobs.[5]

Providing jobs is paramount. With their young and increasingly educated populations, leaders in these commodity-rich countries,

Saudi Arabia especially, need to provide an array of stable and productive employment opportunities to maintain stability and stave off unrest.

Woman in a Strange Land

Of the countries that have been added to emerging market (EM) status over the past decade, Saudi Arabia is the most significant. That made any challenge I experienced on my trip to the seemingly forbidden Kingdom worthwhile. By the time I left Saudi territory, I was convinced that the country would soon "emerge."

Management teams tend to be hungry for flows of capital, and their GCC peers were well on their way to receiving them. Local stock market experts had spent years concerned about the "hot money" invested by hedge funds. These funds would rapidly enter local markets, bid up their stock prices, then just as rapidly divest, leaving businesses hurting for cash and depressing returns for those investors who were willing to stay.

The Saudi authorities were so fearful of this hot money effect that their initial hurdles for investment were restrictive. Their first opening sought exclusively foreign capital from institutional investors with limited turnover and avoided capital from hedge funds, which tend to aggressively chase trades and manage portfolios with high churn. Requirements were set to only allow investors with a track record of five years and at least $1 billion in invested capital. This modest start achieved the goal of testing the waters but prevented the majority of investment funds from accessing the market.

As research by Saudi Arabia's Capital Markets Authority evolved, though, they discovered institutional dollars that were eager to invest in the country, with its vast resources and its large demographic of wealthy young people. Investing in consumer and education companies that targeted this cohort had tremendous potential, such as Almarai (a food and dairy company with the world's highest-yielding cows, attributed to their residing in air-conditioned quarters) and Saudi Telecom Company (offering the largest mobile phone network in a country where the penetration of cell phones is approximately 1.4 per person).[6] As Saudi Arabia fast-forwarded to the future, rich opportunities were cropping up for investing in infrastructure, both real assets and the digital economy. This wasn't a short-term, "hot" theme, but a secular one, and longer-term investors were hooked.

The opportunity to invest in Saudi Arabia was vast. The market offered more than twice the liquidity of all the other frontier markets combined. The companies offered exposure to this nascent market that was positioned to skyrocket with its compelling demographic. In the near term, the opportunity to be early to this market lay open, ahead of the wall of capital that would pour into the country once it was fully liberalized. Basic math confirms that if Saudi Arabia were to be given an "emerging market" classification, the market would rapidly appreciate. Why? Because passive funds, or index funds, represent trillions of dollars, and their mandate is to follow the benchmark. If the benchmark shifts to include a new country, the passive allocations are obligated to shift to reflect the benchmark. For every one dollar of passive money that is invested into a newly upgraded market, approximately five dollars of actively managed capital is invested accordingly. The opportunity was compelling, and I needed to understand if Saudi Arabia was on the brink of an upgrade.

A woman conducting on-the-ground research in Riyadh faces a number of obstacles. In the Introduction to this book, I related how a guard stopped me when I was trying to attend the Saudi Telecom Company (STC) headquarters for an investor meeting. In addition, the investor relations team gave us facts in terms so bureaucratic, it was hard to confirm the idea that brought me there—that the UAE upgrade might be delayed so that the Morgan Stanley Capital International (MSCI) could accommodate Saudi Arabia.

Management teams tend to be great sources of information. I had expected the CFOs and CEOs I met in Saudi, almost all of whom were expats—Americans, Germans, Lebanese—to be the same. But even they couldn't confirm my hunch. Still, I'd seen ample signs amid the Saudi austerity that change was on its way.

Back in the United States, and sensing an impending upgrade, I yearned to buy. It wasn't easy; the country's economy was still entirely closed. I couldn't invest directly in stocks, so I worked with intermediaries who built derivative instruments so that investors like me could access particular securities in which to invest. I pushed ahead, though, and before too long I was running one of the largest US-based investment strategies in Saudi Arabia's stock market.

Three years later, the long-awaited UAE upgrade indeed took place. In 2014, both UAE and Qatar advanced from frontier to emerging market status on the MSCI—the first time in the history of the index that a country was upgraded. From an investment standpoint, it was great news. When frontier countries become emerging ones, they have instant access to a much larger pool of capital. Early frontier investors, including myself, were rewarded. The UAE stock market posted a 99% return from the day that MSCI announced the country's upgrade to the day that it was made effective. It was a momentous event. As a result, the UAE market literally doubled in size.

Saudi Arabia's turn was imminent, but when would it be?

Opening the Doors

The rise of Saudi Arabia's oil empire has led its government to become one of the globe's wealthiest. Its sovereign wealth fund is the fourth largest, following Norway, China, and UAE, just surpassing Kuwait. Saudi Arabia uses these assets to drive development of new sectors and initiatives at home, and it invests heavily abroad, including in the tech sector alongside traditional defense and financials sectors. With this wealthy profile, one may wonder why this country needs foreign capital.

I pursued the answer to this question relentlessly as I entered Saudi investments in 2012. I came to learn of the Saudi authorities' appreciation of a key result of foreign capital. Outside money drives institutionalization, holding businesses accountable, and it demands transparency. Foreign money is also diversified money, limiting the dependency on local financiers and their idiosyncratic investment philosophies. Finally, foreign capital is strategic capital and provides insight on emerging innovative sectors, from FinTech to CleanTech, all areas of strategic interest to the Kingdom.

In short, Saudi Arabia sought the power of international capital, which would ensure stability at home and launch the Kingdom into the heart of the globe's beating capital flows.

Saudi Arabia is but one beneficiary of globalization, which was enabled in part by the groundwork laid by multilateral agencies in the late 1990s. The formation of the World Trade Organization (WTO) broke down barriers and enabled trade across borders to access new resources, labor, and consumers. Further, agencies such as the International Monetary Fund (IMF) and World Bank improved their "development playbook" after the Russian debt crisis and the Asian financial collapse. At that point, they began to emphasize key tenets in stabilizing developing market economies, such as allowing exchange rates to float in order to bear the shocks of boom-bust cycles; building long-term coffers; reducing current-account deficits; and ensuring proper governance standards, such as central bank independence. Prominent countries liberalized their economic policies, allowing foreign investment into their local economies in order to participate in the global fund flows that followed. China is a classic example, given its enormous size.

Other nations have also made significant changes to facilitate liberalization. Saudi Arabia itself, back in June 2013, took the radical step of redefining the country's weekend schedule. It had long been an outlier among Muslim countries, celebrating its weekends on Thursday and Friday (the Islamic day of worship) while other Muslim countries—including its Gulf neighbors—did so on Friday and Saturday.

This momentous change ran counter to centuries of tradition and threatened to disrupt many aspects of Saudi life. But it was a shrewd move. From my perspective, it was designed in part to facilitate the liberalization of the Saudi stock market, which, previously, shared just three working days a week with the prime global markets of the non-Muslim world. By adding another day, the Saudis opened their stock market fully to other GCC nations, as well as foreign investment from outside the Gulf.

In 2014, the Saudi government took another step toward liberalization by announcing that it would open its stock market within one year. It was an audacious move, but they pulled it off. As an experienced Saudi watcher, I wasn't surprised. The move was largely technical; while investors could indeed obtain permitted access, in practice, the infrastructure to execute the trades didn't exist yet. Nevertheless, after fits and starts over several months, the wheels started turning, and investment capital— including my own—poured into the nation.

The measures taken by emerging economies in general to participate in global flows have been remarkably successful. Going back further in history can be instructive. The strategy of economic liberalizing for increased global competitiveness reshaped the planet in the 1990s. At that time, I was an undergraduate student at Stanford, studying under then-Provost Condoleeza Rice. I vividly recall her sharing her experience on the National Security Council, directing

Soviet affairs during the crumbling of the Soviet Bloc. She stressed that social sustainability objectives are best met by good governance and economic liberalization, as the two-way flow of funds fights corruption, improves governance, and enables spending on healthcare and education. Liberalization, not protectionism, increases a country's GDP per capita, distributes wealth, and reduces poverty and, ultimately, inequality.

The end of the Communist bloc was not the only major event that led even skeptics to question the role of state intervention. Emerging economies across the globe adopted these economic reforms as state interventions were increasingly going out of favor. Deng Xiaoping was already "opening up" China, while South Africa's leadership lost credibility as violent protests brought the period of state-led apartheid to an end. For countries that resisted, many found that Margaret Thatcher's "there is no alternative" policy rang true. India, for example, was forced into liberalization following multiple failed attempts and ensuing economic crises. The country faced low reserves, risk of default, and downgraded bond ratings, to the point that even the World Bank and IMF would not back the country. At one point, India faced no option but to airlift the national gold reserves to the IMF to secure financing. This financing came with powerful strings that ultimately unleashed the economy and opened a period of roaring growth.

As countries worldwide embraced privatization of government assets, lower tax rates for business, less restrictions on capital flows, and greater labor flexibility, foreign direct investment (FDI) soared across the globe. The period 1991–2000 marked the fastest growth in FDI in the World Bank's FDI tracking history: a whopping 750% growth.[7]

Increasing worldwide flows came with risk. Emerging markets experienced one of their worst financial shocks in history in the late 1990s when the Asian "tiger economies" (South Korea, Thailand, Malaysia, Indonesia, Singapore, and the Philippines) crashed. These countries were offering the largest growth rates in the world, fueled by their adoption of privatization measures. Investors poured in, leading to soaring real estate values, bold corporate spending, rising correlations (signifying market risk), and frothy markets. When the asset bubble popped, businesses collapsed, the nominal GDP per capita plunged (43% in the case of Indonesia), and millions of people fell below the poverty line. Yet investors were undeterred. If anything, they used this example as a case study about why liberalization strategies, such as a floating exchange rate and an independent central bank, must be adopted.

FDI trends, smoothed over a multiyear horizon, have increased every year until 2016, when some say the world reached "peak globalization." During this period the IMF declared that integration of the world economy had proven to be a "powerful means for countries to promote economic growth, development, and poverty reduction."[8] Integration has raised living standards and increased incomes, to the point that emerging countries represent more than one-half of world trade, up from about a quarter in the early 1970s.

The evidence is clear. As the IMF states, "No country in recent decades has achieved economic success, in terms of substantial increases in living standards for its people, without being open to the rest of the world." Each of the greatest rising countries over the past decade are those that introduced sweeping economic liberalization policies in the 1990s.

By contrast, countries that have resisted the free flow of capital have emerged as case studies in poor governance, with consequences that are economically drastic and socially tragic. While a few countries drawing investments have moved against economic liberalization, investors have resoundingly voted against the others that have.

One such case was Argentina, which showcased the risks of anti-globalist, protectionist policies. The decade began with then-President Christina Kirchner nationalizing YPF—its significant energy company—which essentially stole the capital invested by foreign investors. Capital controls were then introduced to stem the massive outflows from the country that followed this move.

After Kirchner failed in her attempt to revise Argentina's term limits from two years to three, then lost the election to technocrat Mauricio Macri, investors were optimistic. At first, their hope seemed justified. Under Macri's regime, capital controls were removed, and the major benchmarks upgraded the country to emerging. I recall asking Henry Fernandez, the CEO of MSCI, about the rationale at a birthday party for MSCI's 30-year Emerging Markets index at the New York Stock Exchange. He admitted that he hoped the country would not reissue the capital controls. I smiled but remained skeptical.

After only a matter of weeks, the country's weak economic infrastructure caused Macri to reissue capital controls. Investors buckled. Despite shifting policies and transient signs of optimism, Argentina persisted as investors' favorite short of the decade. At the time of this writing, Argentina is once again on a watch list for a potential downgrade.

Other examples of countries that introduced capital controls across this millennium, such as Nigeria, Ukraine, Venezuela, and Zimbabwe, are certainly not shining examples of success. Ukraine's capital controls were introduced following the invasion of eastern Crimea by Russia in 2016 and never reopened. Each of the remaining countries are resource-heavy ones that have suffered disproportionately over the decade.

Perhaps the powers that be in Saudi Arabia were taking notes, because in May 2019, a profound shift occurred. The country was upgraded to an emerging market country, winning MSCI's coveted upgrade and enabling the country to become one of the best market performers on earth. It was an impressive step toward achieving the Kingdom's Vision 2030 economic diversification strategy.

The initial weight in the benchmark was a mere 2.6%, on par with Mexico or Russia, but it was positioned to potentially triple—depending on the rumored IPO of Saudi Aramco.

Crown's Jewel

With this backdrop to provide perspective, it is all the more encouraging that oil-rich countries such as Saudi Arabia and the United Arab Emirates have executed their liberalization strategies. The Gulf countries' efforts during the last decade have paid off, since the majority of the emerging market upgrades were Kuwait, UAE, Qatar, and Saudi Arabia.

I should point out that, while it's well known that macroeconomic growth doesn't always translate into stock market returns, unimpressive returns overseas have left many EM investors dismayed—and investors in domestic stocks feeling validated. At a time when US markets experienced double-digit annualized returns, emerging markets returned a paltry 3%.

But this seemingly lackluster performance is deceptive. If you go below the surface, you see clear trends. First, the period 2010–2020 was a paradoxical ride, with declining performance over the first half followed by a solid rally in the second. Second, the emergence of GCC diversification during the past decade has occurred during a period when energy prices crashed, dropping from $164 a barrel. By 2020, with some traders paying to offload their oil holdings, oil prices literally fell into the negative dollar range. At the same time, some of these oil-exporting nations contained some of the world's best-performing markets. The reason was liberalization.

The opening of Saudi Arabia's stock market in particular was one of the greatest investment stories of the past 10 years. During my Saudi visit in the early 2010s, I noted discreet signs of liberalization. These proliferated after Mohammed bin Salman—known as MBS—was named crown prince in 2017. MBS set out to transform the country at a rapid pace, launching an ambitious aggressive reform agenda, the National Transformation Plan (NTP). It was a move that no one, at least in America, seemed to expect. Doubtless, many Saudis were also taken by surprise. Those expats in senior roles whom I'd met in Riyadh left the country, whether by force, economic pressure, social pressure, or just to seize the next opportunity.

The aims of the NTP are threefold:

1. To diversify the country's dependence on oil. Removing the economic dependency on oil's boom-bust cycles will provide more stable growth and prevent the country from a long-range downturn as the world transitions to a low-carbon economy.

2. To lift the country away from its extremist history. Its social measures reduce the power of the religious police, recognize the value of women in the workforce, and remove the geopolitical fallout of being the largest sponsor of militant global terrorists, including those who launched the attack that forever altered the world's trajectory on September 11, 2001.

3. To open its market to the global economy. Bringing in economic flows can smooth the volatility of the local stock markets and diversify the funding base for ambitious goals such as doubling the contribution of small and midsized businesses and developing a renewables-based, innovation-oriented, tech-driven economy.

A spectacular element of the plan was a proposed IPO of Saudi Aramco, the enormous state-owned oil producer that is the country's crown jewel. This aspect of the plan at first was regarded as a joke in investment circles, at least in the United States, since it seemed inconceivable that any nation could launch an IPO of that size. Further, why would this long-secluded, geopolitically powerful country have any desire to open its crown jewel to foreign ownership? Aramco was widely understood to be the most profitable company in the world. Why open it to public scrutiny?

Over time, speculation grew. Where would the company list? Surely, such a large company couldn't just list locally—it would dominate its own index. The United States couldn't be an answer; the 9/11 trials were still under way. Listing in the United Kingdom would result in too much investor overlap with the local economy. What about China? Could Aramco invest in Shanghai? That seemed too far-fetched, as the onshore market was too nascent for international investment. Besides, if Aramco was looking for Chinese investors, why wouldn't it opt for a strategic alliance and remain private?

Market speculators—confident that the local authorities couldn't build a quick path to liberalization—were proven wrong in 2018, when Saudi Aramco became a publicly listed company. And it listed exclusively in its home market. The company's management listed 5% of Aramco at a valuation of approximately $2 trillion. Locally, it was an immediate hit. As Reuters reported: "From taxi drivers to clerics, Saudis clamoring to own part of state oil giant Aramco went online and to local banks on Sunday at the start of a long-delayed share sale for what could be the world's biggest initial public offering." It was indeed the largest IPO in history.

Overall, the Saudi story is an exemplar of how globalization can create capital. Today, its market still looks good. Although oil prices are falling, the country could get a tailwind, given its current inventories and strong global demand, if and when they begin to rise. Its newfound resilience to this drag shows what foresight can do for an emerging market country.

In addition, a 2019 event underscored the fact that, even in Saudi Arabia, fossil fuels are on the wane. That September, drone attacks damaged two oil installations, ones that processed most of the Saudis' crude oil. Yemen's Houthi rebels took credit for the attacks, which caused extensive damage and threatened to disrupt the world's oil supplies.

This was, of course, huge news. As a keen Saudi watcher, I waited to see how the market would react. To my amazement, it didn't even seem to register with investors. The market hardly budged. Oil, even in the Saudi economy, is on its way to becoming yesterday's news.

Gleam of Success

Saudi Arabia has made so much economic progress since my surreal 2011 visit, when it was both commodity-driven and difficult to access. Yet that does not mask the very real impediments that linger from its past, as the grisly assassination of the Saudi expatriate journalist Jamal Khashoggi in 2018 at the Saudi embassy in Istanbul—allegedly committed at the order of MBS—amply demonstrated.

Despite Saudi's incredible progress over the past decade, challenges remain. Its economy remains heavily dependent on oil. With more reserves than any other country and the lowest cost of production, Saudi Arabia will without a doubt be the "last man standing" as the world shifts toward alternative fuels. Over this period of transition, the country's economic coffers will be inherently tied to the deteriorating demand for oil.

Given the country's huge fiscal reserves, however, economic challenges may be the least of its concerns. Rather, Saudi faces severe sociopolitical dynamics both at home and beyond. Within the country, the Ritz Carlton "blitz" power play by MBS in 2018 showcases the potential rifts and outcomes of a royal family in turmoil. During the corruption crackdown, the crown prince's entourage detained and tortured family members and leading businesspeople. Some considered this step not just a power grab, but also, in fact, an asset grab, as his government extracted $800 billion from personal finance accounts, claiming they were linked to corruption. As an investor, I applaud the anticorruption ideology, but I continue to be concerned about how power will be ceded in the coming years, with the internal feuds and limited judiciary systems.

Saudi Arabia's ability to manage geopolitical feuds is similarly murky. Through the last decade, it has led a vicious war against its Yemeni neighbors, costing the nation both dollars and its reputation in the international sphere, as images of locally starving babies have dominated newswires globally. It has picked questionable fights with surrounding GCC nations as well, including a diplomatic crisis with Qatar in 2017 just as the nation was gearing up for its foreign opening drive.

Still, signs of hope abound in the country. In 2018, Saudi women were given the right to drive. They're beginning to enter the working world, if not in large numbers. At one point, I was approached by one of the royal princesses, HRH Princess Haifa Mohammed Alsaud, to discuss the possibility of bringing NASCAR—of all things!—to her country. Clearly, the Kingdom is undergoing a profound social transformation.

Today Riyadh, the Saudi capital, is filled with gleaming, futuristic-looking skyscrapers—including the dramatically curved Hamad Tower—which sprouted up in a building boom in the years after my trip. The city has modernized at warp speed. It now closely resembles the soaring, prosperous-looking urban centers of its neighbors in the Gulf.

The reality of this new Saudi Arabia was brought home to me in a New York City taxi early in 2020. As we zipped through busy Manhattan streets, I watched distractedly as a long commercial for a luxurious destination, complete with pristine beaches, waving palm trees, and happy couples scuba-diving in azure waters, played out on the video screen on the back of the driver's seat.

To my astonishment, this paradise turned out to be . . . Saudi Arabia! It seemed like a different universe from the place I'd visited just 10 years before. The Saudis in the film were even speaking English! Once closed to tourism, the country can now be entered almost effortlessly, thanks to an e-visa system introduced by MBS.

It was a sharp contrast to the country of a decade ago—and a confirmation that my hunch about the country had been correct.

Saudi's transformation has a significance that extends far beyond its borders. Its breathlessly rapid liberalization, both cultural and economical, portends well for its evolution, as the country transitions from its commodity-dependent past to its tech-driven future. The story also portends well for the future of emerging markets, as less than half have liberalized as of today. As countries globally adopt the policies that integrate markets and release economic shackles, the potential is vast, for both local citizens and international investors alike.

4

Submerging Markets? Corruption and Autocracy

Romania's Unexpected Rise and the Role of Capital Markets

Not so long ago, Romania was being crushed by corruption, and just next door, Turkey was a rising star.

Turkey's eminence stemmed from its long-standing base in democratic principle. Formerly the heart of the Ottoman Empire, it experienced a secular revolution in 1922 that was so extreme, people who refused to abandon the Turkish alphabet for the more Western-friendly Roman one were put to death. Backed by idiomatic "young Turks," Mustafa Kemal Atatürk had a vision of Turkey as a modern, European country, and that included cultural, political, and economic reforms, including banning the wearing of the veil and other symbols of religious affiliation. He afforded rights to women, including full universal suffrage in 1934, and provided free primary education for all Turks. Although with brutal methods, Atatürk united Turkey and propelled it into the modern world.

During the first decade of this century, the country reached a pinnacle of growth under newly elected President Recep Tayyip Erdoğan. As his grasp on power has tightened, however, Turkey has been increasingly plagued by corruption. Ever since his 2014 reelection, there's been an ominous, authoritarian tone to communications by the state. Elections appear to be rigged; dissenting parties have been banned. Censorship of the press and social media is on the rise. Political opponents and journalists—guilty or not—have been imprisoned on shaky grounds.

Money can often see through headlines news though, and Erdoğan aimed to woo these financial guardians. In the midst of this growing repression, I was one of many investors who attended a 2018 meeting with the president. It was a jarring experience. Even presidents are normally polite to groups of top investors because they realize that investment is critical to their country's success. By contrast, Erdoğan brought more armed guards than any head of state I had ever seen. It was clear to me that he wasn't trying to woo investors. Standing across the room beneath a large banner reading "INVEST IN TURKEY," he seemed to be aiming to command us.

Prior to the meeting, President Donald Trump had doubled tariffs on aluminum and steel—Turkey's fourth largest export. Reeling from the blow, Erdoğan demanded that we both maintain our investments in the country and push to relax the tariffs. Shaking his fist in frustration, he hectored us, as if we'd chosen to impose the strictures ourselves. "You cannot wake up from your sleep and just say you've put some new bunch of taxes on steel," he thundered through the interpreter on my headset. "There must be consistency."

His exhortations fell on deaf ears. From a market performance perspective, Turkey has provided disappointment upon disappointment. This country, which once seemed so promising, seems locked in an endlessly negative news cycle. Two years before that, in July 2016, a failed military coup led to a rapid fall in the value of the country's currency. I had the disconcerting experience of witnessing this dramatic event on television. In one montage, fighter jets encircled the capital buildings in Ankara. Then the television flashed images of Turkish soldiers protectively guarding such strategic assets as Taksim Square—the heart of commercial Istanbul—and the Bosphorus Bridge, the span that connects Europe and Asia. The next morning, I learned how the result of this embarrassing theater played out on the public stage. I checked the

Bloomberg terminal to see how the lira, the Turkish currency, was faring. In short order, it collapsed.

As you can imagine, a year later when Erdoğan berated my investor cohort for our "inconsistency" in not investing in Turkey, his demands failed to sway me. His oppressive regime held Turkey under his thumb, but his demands did no more for us than to display his arrogance.

The decade ended with an abysmal currency crisis. By June 2021, the lira was again in freefall, reaching "a fresh low against the dollar and prompting the central bank governor to push back against expectations of an imminent move."[1] Given this economic instability, as well as deteriorating diplomatic ties with the United States and the persistent threat of an internal coup, Turkey had become too volatile for most investors to handle.

In one leader, as in other undemocratic states, is embodied the striking effect when a country's governance shuts down the mechanisms that permit the power of capital to flow. Turkey's fortunes were poised to rise, but after Erdoğan's pursuit of total control, it's become one of the greatest losers of the past decade.

Meanwhile, just to the north, Romania showcases the opposite story. Here, from the dingy ashes of Soviet control has sprung a classic tale in economic freedom. One of the greatest market performers of the last decade, Romania shows what happens when an economy is liberalized. As the country's citizens have blossomed, it has become attractive to foreign investors as well.

Given its small size and corruption-filled headlines during the same first decade, one might have considered this a submerging market. While the country was classified as frontier, it was growing fast. Once its economic progress gathered steam, I yearned to know: Could outside capital help Romania become the next emerging market? I decided to put boots on the ground.

A Sinister Beauty

The Romanian Revolution, which brought independence as the Soviet Bloc collapsed, took place in 1989. Yet during my journey to the country, the past felt like an ominous shadow on the present. Never was it more pronounced than the sunny Saturday when I traveled with my husband, kids, and father for a weekend in the country. We wanted to explore Brașov, a beautiful Transylvanian city of medieval stone houses and narrow cobblestone streets. Transylvania, of course, is the home of the legendary Count Dracula.

Arriving there was an adventure. Our driver steered us through the Carpathian Mountain on a road filled with steep turns, looping curves, and lurching descents. Our driver remarked cheerfully about the views of Bâlea Lake along the route. I didn't see any of them. I had my eyes tightly shut as we screeched around switchbacks. For once I understood the expression of finding one's heart in one's throat.

To reward ourselves on arrival, we ate lunch in a sunny café, ending with a sweet order of *papanasi*, a mouth-watering rich donut topped with cream and blueberry jam. As we walked outside, I sat our restless boys and packed bag on a bench so I could snap photos of the gold-tinted building. When I turned around, I discovered the boys playing in the adjacent field—but the backpack gone. It contained our passports, computers, iPhones, and iPads, including my firstborn's baby pictures (at a time when the cloud hadn't yet been invented!), my reading glasses, jewelry, and more.

As we reported the theft to the authorities, the police station provided a forbidding sense of having entered the country's socialist past. While my father kept the boys outside, an officer demanded that I write down by hand a report of the crime. He glowered at me as he dictated what he thought it should say. His colleagues, unsmiling, stared at me pitilessly. My hand shook with fear as I wrote.

Another officer insisted to view the scene of the crime with my husband. As they walked to the police car, I overheard him say severely to Nikhil, "This is your fault."

This incident came to sum up Romania's heritage for me. It was just a petty theft, and these do happen all over the world. Nevertheless, our visit to the police station, with the jaded, cynical cops in attendance, encapsulated a sense that I would have all through our trip. Romania was a place of extravagant beauty, with exquisite medieval towns and glorious landscapes. Plus, I was drawn there because it was the second-fastest growing country on the continent. Yet Romanian life had an austere edge. Fear and anxiety remained, long after communism was banished.

From Brasov we rode back to Bucharest on a lumbering, antiquated train. All five of us, downbeat and tired after the day's drama, fell asleep soon after we climbed on board. Both boys, seated on either side of their grandfather, slept soundly, lulled by the movement of the train; the head of each one leaned against one of their *nana's* shoulders.

After arriving at Bucharest's Gara Nord, we hailed a taxi for the trip to our hotel. Here too we were surrounded by glimpses of the past. We passed blockish concrete buildings—classic Soviet architecture—but also beautiful Beaux Arts structures that looked as if they'd been airlifted from France. No wonder Bucharest is known as the "Little Paris of the East." (It even has a copy of that city's famous Arc de Triomphe, if significantly smaller.)

On a more petty scale, Romania's past showed its hold on its citizens. During our five-minute trip we were ripped off three separate times, by two different taxi drivers, before we reached our hotel. I shouldn't have been surprised: Romania has a reputation for endemic bribery and corruption. Both were commonplace during the country's communist years, notably under the notorious dictator Nicolae Ceaușescu, the last president of the Socialist Republic of Romania. These long years were marked by hardship, food shortages, and deep corruption.

That changed after Romania's 1989 revolution, one of the waves that took place within the USSR satellites in Eastern Europe. By the time it was over, Ceaușescu had been executed, and communist rule was ended. Still, changing a country's culture occurs only over a period. As one of my taxi drivers ironically remarked, "Corruption has replaced communism as the plague of Eastern Europe."

As a young analyst, I was covering the Romanian market at the time of the country's admission to the EU. I was skeptical, feeling it had been admitted too soon. After all, less than a decade had passed since the fall of Ceaușescu. The country's economy was in terrible shape. Joining the EU could bring benefits that would enhance its governance, from European investments and regulation to a bloc-wide commitment to stamping out corruption.

One specific advantage of EU membership was the ability of the European Commission to keep tabs on Romania's governance-related issues. Both Romania and Bulgaria were admitted on the condition that they submit to monitoring by the EU until they advanced firmly toward judicial reform. These transitional measures, known as the Cooperation and Verification Mechanism (CVM), remain in place today.

Symbols of extreme wealth, wildly disproportionate to most of the population, remained. The great gulf between the country's rulers and its ordinary citizens was conspicuous. The most obvious of these was the Palace of Parliament, the world's second-largest administrative building (after the Pentagon), described in my Lonely Planet guide as "Ceauşesco's most infamous creation."[2] Construction on this behemoth—which measures 3,552,090 square feet and has more than 3,000 rooms—began in 1984. It's still not complete.

As the work week began, I embarked on a round of meetings alongside other investors. We first visited the country's Ministry of Economy Trade and Business Environment. We crammed into a small elevator and pushed the clear button until it lit orange. When we exited, I was startled to find the office space vast and undecorated. The office furniture was clunky and utilitarian, with rarely a framed picture to break the monotony of the endless white walls. We were shown to a large room with black polyester carpet and white tables upon aluminum frames, reminding me of furniture in an underfunded public school building.

It was enlightening to hear both the investors' concerns and the leaders' responses. Some members of my group expressed their frustration with the privatization process, saying that the transfer of power and property from the government into the hands of the people hadn't gone far enough.

Remus Vulpescu, who was then an advisor to the Ministry, was startlingly frank in his responses. He told us that Romania risked becoming a "degenerated republic," a place where corruption was rampant.

I reminded him, "Your authorities just arrested so many officials and business people in the corruption crackdown."

"Yes, we arrested 1,000 people," he agreed. Then he coldly added, "That wasn't enough."

From Hard Communism to Hard Capitalism

On the other hand, accusations of corruption can be a political weapon as well. How can you know who's really corrupt and who isn't? Our family friend Stefan Lungu has, for example, been arrested multiple times. In 2017, Romania's High Court of Cassation and Justice[3] sentenced him to parole after a bribery investigation found former Tourism Minister Elena Udrea guilty of taking bribes and abuse of office. She was ordered to spend six years in jail. Stefan had been her advisor.

Our own sentiments were that we were lucky to have Stefan as our insider. He was a well-traveled friend who, along with his beautiful family, is so well known in Romania that they've become tabloid fodder. Stefan once headed the Department of Tourism himself, and he designed its modern, inviting logo—a friendly green leaf that references both the country's breathtaking Transylvanian Alps and its sustainable future. A self-described artist, Stefan's jovial free spirit contrasted sharply with the somber Bucharest's historic city center.

Stefan graciously picked up our family from our hotel to escort us to the greener outskirts. On our walk, we took turns identifying traces of Soviet-era austerity. Some were amusing, such as restaurants named, simply, "Restaurant" and stores named, you guessed it, "Store"—holdovers from a communist past where conformity was a virtue.

In addition, I noted the severity of daily life in Romania. Its citizens seemed reserved, cautious about what they said—another holdover from communist days, when so many were under surveillance. I noticed that even Stefan, typically ebullient, at times looked fearful, reminding me of the jittery journalist in Hanoi.

In our encounters with shopkeepers and restauranteurs, I could feel an edge of reticence. While usually pleasant and polite, they seemed suspicious, as if they assumed we were spies. Even Romanians who weren't alive at the time of Soviet rule had retained a kind of muscle memory of that repressive experience.

Romania's recent past is a gory one. In World War II, the Romanian government colluded with Nazi Germany, subjugating and killing hundreds of thousands of its own population, primarily Jewish and Roma. The country then suffered defeat at the hands of the Allied powers, which bombed Romania to stop Nazi advances in Europe, and the Soviet Union, which seized territory from Romania and ruled the country for decades after. Back in its communist days, Romanian citizens were known to turn on each other, reporting people to the authorities for crimes, real or imagined. People could disappear without a trace.

All through my time in Romania I had the same, persistent thought—something terrible happened here. All those centuries of violence had left a complicated legacy behind.

The French influences and Byzantine architecture, combined with the air of intrigue, suspicion, and uncertainty permeating the city, created a unique blending of two distinct cultures that appeared at turns throughout our travels. At times, the idea that Bucharest was a Little

Paris didn't fit at all. Stefan joked with me, "What if Paris had an affair with Moscow?" he teased. "Bucharest would be the result."

All through our travels, I kept one singular objective in mind. *Could the country's new link to the West accelerate its upgrade to emerging status?*

Like other former USSR satellites, Romania faced numerous challenges as it emerged from communism, but it has fared far better. For one, Romania has been able to readily integrate with its capitalist neighbors due to the roots of its language, which it shares with others in Western Europe. As I knew from Vietnam and other countries, communication is far easier among languages that share the same alphabet.

Furthermore, Romania advanced in part due to the fact that its relationship with the USSR was more adversarial than other Eastern Bloc countries. There were episodes of fierce anticommunist resistance in Romania when it was under Soviet rule. Plus, its post-communist government embraced capitalist principles more readily than did many of its neighbors.

Guided, in part, by the International Monetary Fund (IMF), the new government took radical steps to reduce the role of the state, privatizing some companies and nationalizing others. It also disbanded state-owned enterprises, which, to this day, make up about 40% of the companies. Other nations, such as Slovenia, which split from Yugoslavia in 1991, took a more gradual approach to private-sector development—"It was soft communism, now it's soft capitalism," one Bucharest cab driver told me—and their economies lagged as a result.

Later that afternoon, I tapped on the door of the office of Guillermo Tolosa, a Uruguayan who served as the IMF's regional representative. I was surprised to learn that, though South American, he had been stationed in Romania for some time. He eagerly greeted me and invited me to sit.

Guillermo was impassioned by Romania's prospects. As we sat in stiff chairs facing each other, he spoke enthusiastically of the abundant opportunities. Waving his arms for emphasis, he posed a rhetorical question: "Why is the Bucharest IKEA open 24 hours a day?"

The answer, he shared, was that young people were anxious to buy day *and* night, 24/7. (Privately, I noted with amusement, the contrast between his extravagant gestures and this Swedish retailer's low-key, minimalist aesthetic.) The local IKEA store was indeed open all day and night back then—a rarity for the international chain.

He explained that the IMF views the nation's dynamic, energetic youth as eager to share in wealth, consumerism, and other rewards of capitalism. Guillermo then made a point that really caught my attention. While discussing Romania's development, he made reference to the Latin American country of Colombia, citing the historic success of its stock market.

What was their secret? "Public equity can be a vehicle to deliver FDI [foreign direct investment]," he said. "Markets are an excellent way to drive prosperity and economic growth." I couldn't have said it better myself.

Sustainable Markets

A working vacation has its drawbacks. That night I holed up in our hotel room's bathroom so my boys and husband could sleep in the adjoining dark bedroom. In the stillness I studied my notes from the day.

Positioning my laptop on the bathroom floor, I found Romania's IMF package online. I plowed into the thick file. Sure enough, Provision 6 of this massive multilateral document, shared primarily among bureaucrats and policy wonks, referenced the equity capital markets. The terms required Romania to invest in its market and drive liquidity.

So there it was, in black and white. It was as if Guillermo's words from earlier in the day were staring back at me from the page, only translated into bureaucratic legalese. Romania's commitment to development included developing its stock market.

This notion runs counter to some sustainability rhetoric today. Some believe that market mechanisms underserve vast populations, since they perpetuate the success of yesterday's winners—especially those who designed the system itself. However, in Romania, where basic needs have been so dire, I saw how markets could create a path to alleviating poverty. For one, the strength of a market mechanism is its unrelenting transparency. Management teams have no choice but to report the sources and uses of their cash, for example. Does that permit room for fraud? Of course, but vast sums can't be swept away as easily as when a company is never obligated to share how its capital is transferred and who is paid what.

In addition, the IMF documents noted, equity markets draw a broader pool of people into a company's economic success. Companies sell ownership rights to public equity shareholders, and this can be considered a path to wealth distribution, assuming the initial shares are accessible at a reasonable price.

Further, equity markets offer an opportunity for investors to infuse liquidity in compelling companies that are creating innovative products that solve real unmet needs, thereby creating jobs and building productive economies.

In sum, public stock markets are ecosystems that reward efficiency, promote innovation, and require transparency. Their mechanisms punish waste, obsolescence, and corruption.

While it was rewarding to see my life's work in a positive light, first and foremost, I had a fiduciary duty to maximize risk-adjusted returns for my investors. An upgrade in status to emerging markets could be a phenomenal driver of returns. I needed to do more detective work to uncover some answers.

After I awoke in the morning, inspired by the prior night's bathroom reading, I walked to the office of the Bucharest Stock Exchange (BSE). Little did I know, I would find just the answers I needed to my critical investment questions.

Daniela Serban, then the BSE's investor relations director, met me at the door. She was a tall blonde woman wearing a modern, stylish suit. We met cordially, while the flashing lights of the TVs throughout the lobby showed the energy and price movements of the exchange. She walked me to a large office and introduced me to the company's CEO, Ludwik Sobolewski, an intense redheaded Polish man.

I soon learned that his interests and mine were aligned. After he presented his company's performance and strategic objectives, I asked him, "Will you seek emerging market status for your country?"

He took a sip from his hot tea and grew emboldened. I had struck a nerve. He pointed first at Daniela and then at others walking the floor of the office. "Look at Romania's potential," he said. "These are young, modern people. They are outraged by the past and determined to set a better path."

In frustration, he exclaimed, "How can Hungary, Czech, and Poland be emerging market countries, while Romania remains merely frontier?"

Ludwik and Daniela acknowledged the challenges. They emphasized the importance of good governance and transparency. "We are in the early days of building corporate governance," Ludwik admitted. I was well aware. One frustrating example for a shareholder like me—shareholder meetings were sometimes announced on the very day they were to be held, although the law requires that there be 30 days between the two events. I was pleased to learn later that Daniela went on to become the president and co-founder of the Romanian Investor Relations Association.

Ludwik knew that an upgrade meant more than prestige. He has tirelessly encouraged companies to go public, listing themselves on the stock exchange and allowing locals to participate in the company's ownership. He explained, reasonably, "After they list, their companies are rewarded by investors. High-quality, high-growth businesses can then thrive"—he looked at me with a wink—"thanks to an expanding set of international investors, eager to support their growth."

Financial Returns and Financial Inclusion

In the months that followed, Romania's stock market soared, making Romania one of the great winners of the past decade. I became more hopeful that Romania would catch the attention of the ratings agencies and achieve an upgrade.

The notion of utilizing the stock exchange to promote the economy and drive innovation was well accepted within Romania. In 1995, just around when the country became an associated state of the EU, the government made a shrewd, tactical decision to reestablish the BSE, which had previously been shuttered for half a century.

After the BSE re-opened, Romania went on to initiate a remarkably successful mass privatization program. From that point on, the country roared ahead, becoming known in the early 2000s as "the Tiger of Eastern Europe." By 2017, it was the fastest growing economy on the continent. As the government liberalized, Romania's progress accelerated, opening new sectors, such as energy and telecoms, to competition and investment.

The country's stock market did more than build an economy and reward investors. It also created a path to restitution. During the communist years, the government had confiscated property from thousands of victims. How could they be repaid?

In 2006, the new government established Fondul Proprietatea to compensate people abusively expropriated. Rather than attempting to reimburse citizens for the value of their lost property, the government offered shares of this fund to the victims. At distribution, the value of the shares matched the actual value of lost property that wasn't returned. The reason for offering shares instead of cash was that the people could share in the country's growth. The fund owns minority stakes in the country's major energy and infrastructure assets, stakes that have been safeguarded to ensure profitability and payouts to investors. As the companies grew more profitable, victims of yesterday's crimes would be paid at today's prices. Romania found a unique, powerful, and effective way to resolve social ills through market mechanisms.

As frontier economies like Romania posted impressive gains, they came to attract the attention of the mainstream press, including esteemed journalist Dan Keeler, founder and writer of The Frontiers column of the *Wall Street Journal*. While Dan's readers would be interested in the return profile of these countries, surely they'd need to be informed on the risks. In Romania, the key risks, it seemed, were governance related.

Dan invited me to join a panel to discuss the importance and process of due diligence in frontier markets. At the time I was running one of the larger frontier funds. While I was honored to be considered, I didn't think I was the right person for the panel. I explained, "I don't conduct deep due diligence on my Romanian holdings or, indeed, any other frontier or emerging ones. My process is quantitative." Dan took some time to take in the information. *How can one stomach the risk of a frontier investment without deep diligence?* he likely wondered. The strength of a quantitative approach is breadth, not depth—the ability to cover 5,000 stocks in frontier markets and evaluate them on dozens of characteristics. I could not, however, visit each company, count the inventory in their backrooms, try out each product, and call supply chain managers to check for fraud or misconduct.

"Dan," I said, "it's not too late to back out." But he insisted that I take part.

To prepare, I looked up the 10 greatest scandals over the past five years, then checked my holdings. To my delight, I discovered that I hadn't owned *any* of the troubled investments. By systematically following the cash flows and running simple checks on governance measures, my portfolios had remained scandal-free. So there it was, to my surprise—living proof that companies with prudent, sustainable practices are rewarded with ample capital.

While proving that proper governance drives returns is straightforward, improving governance standards is a different matter entirely. I learned this first-hand during an investor gathering with then Romanian President Klaus Werner Iohannis.

The meeting's format was surprisingly intimate, a striking contrast to the dinner with Turkish President Erdoğan. My investor meeting was structured as a roundtable—a working group session—with smaller tables pushed together to form literally one round table. The 20 of us in attendance included some of the world's leading investors. The president kept his opening remarks brief, and he earnestly requested our pragmatic feedback. Ideas were discussed and questions fired in rapid succession, while President Iohannis listened, scratching notes into a notebook at each passing comment.

At one point, an investor, and a good friend of mine, commended him on the strides he had made clamping down on corruption in Romania. President Iohannis spoke frankly about the country's recent anticorruption drive, which had had a rocky debut. The year before, riots had erupted in the streets. A thousand demonstrators were arrested after the government moved to change an existing law so that officials convicted of corruption might be freed. The president had sided with the protestors.

My friend went on to explain that, regarding corruption, it's important not to stamp it out too quickly or aggressively. "Corruption," he explained, "is the oil that greases the wheels." None of us wanted to see Romania come to a screeching halt.

Since that time Romania's governments have toppled repeatedly in "a cascade of corruption scandals and political chaos."[4] By 2017, the country had had enough—500,000 citizens demonstrated in cities across Romania after the state threatened to roll back its anticorruption drive. The government backed down.

Biutiful Bucharest

By the end of the week, my family and I met with Stefan on the banks of Herestrau Lake. I had long since shrugged off my lost backpack. All of us were rested and reenergized. Inspired by Romania, I marveled at the green shoots of opportunity that were visible all around me. Through my tinted sunglasses I could see the country's sunny, thriving economy in action.

We happily explored the gardens, stopping finally at our destination, a restaurant called—no kidding—not stoic "Restaurant" but rather more aptly "Biutiful by the Lake." Built on a large floating terrace at the edge of shimmering waters, Biutiful lived up to its name. To the delight of our sons, it overlooked a half-submerged automobile in the center of the lake. With a cocktail menu offering such up-scale, trendy beverages as Liquid Speed by Porsche and Ginger Byzantine, the place was clearly targeted at Bucharest's trend-setting demographic.

I was encouraged by the energetic youth around me. This cohort was responsible for bolstering Romania's consumer base. I thought back to the executives in leadership positions that I'd met in the country, from business leaders to advisors to the president. Most seemed younger than 45. Surely this made Romania's leadership one of the youngest in the world? Today's Romania is a modern capitalistic story.

Biutiful by the Lake's name may sound generic, but its grilled halloumi and capsicum were spicy and unique. When the bill arrived, I found another reason to be impressed. You could pay it electronically—even back then, in a country not long removed from socialism. I saw this modern, tech-enabled, ahead-of-its-time system as a very good sign.

I ticked down a list of other reasons to be optimistic about Romania. I had noticed the surprising prevalence of women and youth in leadership positions and the tangible presence of expats in the country, people who had come both to drive their own careers and make a difference in the country. Even the saga of our lost backpack in Brasov took a positive turn: after our lunch with Stefan, we headed to the US embassy, where we were impressed by the speed and efficiency with which our passports were reissued—within an hour and hassle free.

Romania is now a top performer across all markets. The value of the US dollar has doubled, and at 6%, that nation's compound annual growth rate leads *all* emerging markets. "After 4.8% growth in 2016, Romania recorded an accelerated 6.9% economic growth in 2017, the largest growth rate after the economic crisis and one of the largest in the world," according to Romania's *Voluntary National Review*[5] of its progress on sustainability.

What are the leading factors in Romania's remarkable success? Market liberalization and economic freedom. The latter is measured by the right of citizens to own their own property and benefit from their own labor. Romania has advanced both of these rights and also opened its market and modernized government integrity. Monetary freedom encourages prosperity and helps to create healthier societies.

It brought to mind a memory of 15 years before my Romanian trip, when I was an undergraduate. I studied the words of Hernando de Soto, the Peruvian economist who argued that conferring property rights on the poor would benefit everyone. Ownership provides transparency and clarity, de Soto argued, thereby encouraging investments and raising a nation's level of economic activity.

In Romania, I watched in fascination as de Soto's thesis played out before my eyes.[6] Its impressive economic development, with outstanding market returns and economic growth, had led to significant social progress. Living conditions have improved dramatically, with a concomitant reduction in domestic poverty. The standard of governance has also been raised. Romania is now a thriving democratic state—so much so that, by 2016, the year after our visit, the Human Development Index added it to the list of nations with very high human development.[7]

Castle in the Sky?

In September 2020—the 25th anniversary of the relaunch of the BSE—it happened. Romania was upgraded on the FTSE index from frontier to secondary emerging market status. This move opened the country's capital market to emerging markets funds, while also increasing the visibility of the BSE and locally listed companies.[8]

At the time of this writing, Romania is still looking for an upgrade by Morgan Stanley Capital Index, the index tracked by most institutions.

This raises an important point in the shift that has occurred with emerging markets. For so long, Western countries have thought in terms of foreign aid. Yet what people in developing countries need is not aid, but capital. As these Romanian leaders spoke of their concerns, I saw what a vital role markets play in serving as a source of accountability and transparency. The latter can bring all manner of good governance to bear—by such accessible, low-tech methods as using standardized accounting procedures and providing regular disclosures to investors.

So much of Romanian life has been regarded in the framework of its brutal past. The shadow cast by a fifteenth-century prince known as Vlad the Impaler has colored our perceptions that Romania is somehow still mired in the days of Count Dracula. Of course, as inveterate travelers, we couldn't resist a peek at the ghost of so much gloom and doom.

On the last day of our trip, the idea of visiting the blood-sucking, bat-like monster at his home in Transylvania appealed to all three generations of our family. We ventured up a terrifying road in the direction of Bran Castle, a gloomy fourteenth-century structure with soaring, red-roofed Gothic towers. Our sons, Jasper and Griffen, shivered in ecstatic terror as we ascended the steep stone steps to the castle's entrance.

It's said that if you knock three times on the castle's enormous mahogany door, a bloodthirsty creature, long teeth and all, will let you in.

We knocked decisively—one, two, three.

When the door, slowly, began to open, my whole family held our breath. The boys squealed in fear as the door opened to reveal . . . a mild-mannered employee, without vampire teeth, who informed us that the castle was closed.

As he gently shut the heavy, ornately decorated door, it seemed that the door had shut on Romania's sinister past as well.

5

Terrorism and Instability

When Markets Become Uninvestable: North Africa and the Middle East

Just a few short years ago, I could see absolutely no problem with taking the kids to Ukraine. My husband, however, was dead set against it. In 2014, Russia seized the Crimea and incited pro-Russian forces in the eastern provinces. Fighting in the Donbas region has been ongoing since then. "It's just not safe." The events of 2022 proved him right. We would not have wanted to be on the streets of Kyiv on the day Russia decided to invade the entire country.

Instead, we decided to take the family to Tunisia, the beautiful North African coastal country romanticized by the ancient Greeks and William Shakespeare. That choice became one of my greatest mistakes. That's because a country doesn't have to suffer a full-out war in order to discourage investment. Terrorism of a much smaller order can kill foreign interest.

On the first day we wandered the cobblestoned streets of Sidi Bou Said, a magical town at the edge of the Mediterranean's sapphire blue sea. This village is famously beautiful, with pristine, ivory-colored houses and doors and window grilles of bright cobalt blue. Picturesque tilework—a Tunisian specialty—with floral motifs of pale yellow and blue, lines its doorways, sidewalks, and fountains.

We spent the night, our first in the country, in a beautiful shell-tinted home with a large courtyard. We soon learned that the owner of the inn was a colleague of Nikhil's at AOL several years before. The evening air smelled of the sea and freshly laundered cotton dried by natural heat and sunlight. The next day we set out to explore Sidi Bou Said's main street, darting in and out of its charming small shops, shopping for tiles and colorful mosaics to send to family back home. A street seller stopped us and, in an aggressive yet charming way, tried to convince us to take home an owl. The bird was wonderfully tame and even posed for a photograph while sitting on my husband's head. We burst into laughter, as did the seller. Unfortunately, we couldn't really imagine getting it through customs, even if we did want a live owl.

Very few investors had toured North Africa in recent years, deterred by the region's volatility. But hope was palpable in Tunisia at the time of our visit. Three years had passed since the Arab Spring had erupted—first in Tunisia, then all through the Middle East. This movement had brought a tentative form of democracy along with it. Here, at least, that seemed to have held.

The Arab Spring began in Tunis in December 2010, after the self-immolation of a street vendor, Mohammed Bouazizi, in protest after government officials confiscated the stand where he sold fresh vegetables. With the power of social media technology, images of Bouazizi's fiery death ricocheted around the world and set off a firestorm of protests across the Middle East.

Tunisians had suffered numerous indignities, and worse, under the brutal authoritarian regime of President Zine El Abidine Ben Ali during his 20 years in power. The uprising, initially known as the Jasmine Revolution, proved to be contagious. Protestors took to the streets "with a rock in one hand, a cell phone in the other," as Al Jazeera described it.

Two months later, President Ben Ali fled the country. The movement gathered force. A week or so after that, coordinated demonstrations erupted in Cairo's Tahrir Square; other so-called "Days of Rage" followed in other Arab lands, including Bahrain, Libya, Yemen, and Syria. In the years since, though, these latter two countries erupted in civil wars while most of the other Arab Spring nations slid back into authoritarianism.

While the Egyptians succeeded in unseating their feared dictator, Hosni Mubarak and even held democratic elections for Parliament, it didn't last. Less than a year later, the country's new president, Mohamed Morsi, elected in June 2012, was removed from power by a coup.

Tunisia had started the revolution, and the people were determined to see it through. It was a proud country, with a grand and ancient history. The next day we drove to Tunis to spend the afternoon at the Bardo National Museum. Built in the nineteenth century as an Ottoman palace, the Bardo has been transformed and modernized. The museum today is a bright white rectangular building with a row of classical round Arab arches running along its ground floor.

When we arrived, we came upon a group of security guards sleeping in folding chairs, their heads drooping. Each one incongruously cradled a Kalashnikov assault rifle in his lap. While the presence of weapons was alarming, the tableau seemed like a scene out of a screwball comedy— more amusing than threatening. We entered the museum, and our kids skipped ahead. We were tourists, curious and enthusiastic about what we might find in this quiet, welcoming sanctuary.

Its collection, mainly derived from archeological excavations undertaken in the country, contains the largest collection of Roman mosaics in the world. Its exhibit spaces illustrate the history of Tunisia, ranging from prehistory to the early Christian era and, later, the Islamic one.

The museum features one glorious antiquities-packed gallery after another, including its cloistered Carthage Room, lined with statues from ancient Rome. The jewels of its collection included a third-century one showing *The Odyssey*'s Ulysses resisting sirens trying to lure him onto the rocks. Our boys raced through these spaces, delighted by such unexpected sights as comical terra cotta masks with grinning faces.

Our Bardo visit was a highlight of our North African trip. So imagine our shock when we heard the terrible news in the spring of 2015— only weeks after we visited. On March 18, gunmen staged an armed assault at the Bardo that killed 22 visitors and injured 42 others. Most of the victims were foreign tourists. The attack took place at the museum entrance; other visitors, attempting to flee, were taken hostage. I watched the television news in horror, switching from one channel to another while simultaneously keeping an eye on Twitter for real-time reports. When a tweet flashed by stating that some tourists were shot as they stepped down from the bus from central Tunis to the Bardo, I recalled stepping down from a bus very much like it—with my family.

I was on edge for weeks. I couldn't stop thinking of the lives lost that day, the innocent tourists who were butchered. As for my business interest, I had felt so much promise for Tunisia. I knew that its economy would be devastated as a result of this attack because foreign aid and investment would wane.

Sure enough, Tunisia's economy flatlined. It became a textbook example of how a financial sector is impacted when terrorism breaks out in a country. Before the bombing, Tunisian citizens had accrued more investment power than ever. In its aftermath, with the loss of foreign investment, they lost all their gains. The economy couldn't grow. No IPOs could take place. This emerging economy was stifled.

The circumstances in Tunisia were bleak. In the ensuing months, each time I rebalanced my portfolio away from the country, the faces of the people I had met would flash before me: my smiling, optimistic broker; the convenience-store salesman who surprised my boys with apple-flavored lollipops; the budding entrepreneur who reinvented the diaper to free up women from the monotony of work and expand their opportunities. And those women themselves? What would become of them?

The human component of my investments simultaneously excites and haunts me. As a return-driven investor, I invest in tomorrow's winners and provide countries the essential capital to enable their success. What happens when the conditions are too dire to back them? How can they access capital to escape their cycles of poverty and destruction?

Buying When There's Blood in the Streets

Emerging markets are typically high-growth investment opportunities. The stock markets are composed of companies, founded by entrepreneurs who are determined to serve some need or fill some niche. This is the same as in all markets, but in emerging markets, almost by definition, the unmet needs are vast. Foreign capital can provide infusions that produce growth across a wide spectrum.

Given the geopolitical risks and external dependencies, these investments are often risky. Prices can be volatile, so investors tend to trade for bargains that can't be found in more heavily trafficked developed markets. For an astute investor, these variability factors suggest a compelling investment. Not only are they high growth, but the country-specific risks can be diversified. The opportunity to deliver dynamic effects locally is outsized.

For the investor, the ability to beat the market is outsized as well. Participants in these markets are often local and less sophisticated than those in developed markets, where institutional investors are particularly active. In emerging markets, investors often invest more on local news and are less sensitive to global themes. The scenario for shrewd foreign capital is optimum. The benefits for the local market are maximized. It's a win-win all around.

The question is: how does one generate these returns?

"Buy when there's blood in the streets" is a maxim that I learned during my earliest ventures into emerging markets. Senior portfolio managers would coach me to buy into cheap positions just after a geopolitical event had occurred. They were themselves among the earliest investors in emerging markets, and quite often they were right.

This byword is the essence of the traditional emerging-market handbook, otherwise known as "contrarian investing." Value-oriented investors aim to buy stock themes in environments when they're cheap. Buying when there's volatility and noise is a risky proposition, one that obliges investors to cut through headlines and politics. It can also bring rewards. A cataclysmic event, such as an earthquake or a coup d'état, can cause stock prices to plummet. If an investor sees that the economy could normalize in short order, it can be a great buying opportunity. As Tunisia's story illustrates, however, that wisdom has its limits.

Regions all over the world have their own bloody histories with terrorism. One gruesome and heavily publicized event occurred farther east, in Pakistan. Journalists across the globe were horrified when one of their own, *Wall Street Journal* reporter Daniel Pearl, was brutally beheaded in the country in 2002. The grisly killing was not only a personal tragedy. Tourism and business in the country dried up as a result, as travelers feared for their safety. The event highlights that violence, or even just the threat of it, makes investors shy away.

Years after the beheading event, MSCI kicked Pakistan out of its MSCI Emerging Market Index. While a technical issue drove the downgrade,[1] investors did not protest. As Pakistan fought its way back to investability status, one criterion frequently worked against the country's case: investors were not clamoring to invest there. Few were willing to visit.

As a portfolio manager, I was emboldened by my objectivity. Using computer-based methods, I identified that stocks were trading cheaply and the perceived impact of "blood on the streets" was overestimated. A decade after Daniel Pearl's death, while the shadows lived on, Pakistan had progressed.

One day that year, I was running a perfunctory portfolio rebalance, which occurred at regular intervals. My team ran our investment models to determine what our "optimal" portfolio would look like. On this particular day, the valuation signals suggested that we should load capital into the Karachi Stock Exchange. While the market presented dozens of attractive stocks from across sectors, from banking to fertilizers, I was surprised by the extent of the attractive signal. As I investigated, I came to quickly learn that the Pakistani Supreme Court had just ordered the arrest of the country's prime minister, Raja Pervaiz Ashraf, on corruption charges. The Karachi Stock Exchange plunged.

I reacted cautiously. I wondered if this extreme event could warrant overriding our model—one that's built on a series of historical backtests and simply can't account for every event. After some deliberation, I concluded that the news was simply that—headline news. It was a political event and the impact on the economy would be negligible over the following months.

It was a big risk to go overweight while there was metaphorical blood in the streets, but it was the right decision. The prime minister's arrest order was rescinded the next day. Pakistan turned out to be among the strongest market performers in the months that followed.

Several years later, in May 2017, Pakistan was finally readmitted to the Emerging Market classification by MSCI. On its upgrade, the returns soared, and early investors were rewarded. The contrarian investment strategy had worked.

The case of Pakistan demonstrates the volatility that is present in so many emerging-market countries. Should an investor wait for markets to recalibrate, or should withdrawals be taken? A prudent investor cannot put money into a market without full confidence that that capital will be returned. This underscores the necessity for stable governance—because a country's people will be the ones who suffer from disinvestment. The return of the Taliban to ruling Afghanistan—and once again making women second-class citizens—is only one glaring example. What investor wants to be associated with them?

Another somber example occurred closer to Tunisia. As our family continued on our tour of the MENA (Middle East North Africa) region, our connecting flight was in Beirut. It was familiar ground, for I had invested in Lebanon for many years. Yet in 2019, tumultuous large-scale protests occurred in the streets of the city as state-based conflicts within the larger Middle East hung a dark gray cloud over the picturesque city, what some call the "Paris of the East." In August that year, the Israeli military carried out airstrikes against a Syria-backed Palestinian militant group. The massive destruction forced all major institutional banks to close their Beirut offices. Without a physical presence to keep financial assets secure, international investors were prevented from investing capital locally. As a result, investing was out of the question.

Ultimately, the ongoing unrest and threats of war constrain investments, constrict liquidity, and prevent prosperity from taking root. Instability reaches down into the lives of all a country's citizens, suppressing innovation, peace, and prosperity. So there lies the crux of the matter: investors like risk, but they won't bet on bad actors.

Capital as a Weapon of War

From Beirut, my family flew to Amman, Jordan. Our first stop was to visit with family friends. On a tour through the city, the Al Farah family drove us by the local chocolate factory that they owned and offered fresh tastes to us all. We then visited their home for lunch.

I delighted in the peace of their breathtaking hillside home. It was a modest house surrounded by the steep hills of the floral Levant Mountains. We breathed the fresh sweet fragrance of the local olive, cedar, and eucalyptus trees. Before dinner, I sat with my friend's mother as she flattened balls of dough with her bare hands, tossed, and flipped them against her hot *sat* (domed iron oven) until she formed gently browned *shrak*, the leavened bread of the Bedouin people. When she finished her baking, she brought us to her large dining table, set for a feast to host her family and mine, two dozen in total. We ate in their living room, made cozy with a dozen reclining chairs against the walls and the children eating on the floor in front. We savored the fresh grape leaves, lemon-infused tabouleh, savory falafel, and, of course, Mrs. Al Farah's *shrak*.

The next day, we drove to the family's other factory, located north of Amman, in a historic town called Irbid. As our driver passed alongside the gates to cross the border, I shuddered in horror as I read the sign: *Caution. Entry to Syria.* This was not a welcome sign but rather a patrolled, fenced, and heavily protected border. The guards would not admit visitors at this post.

I asked our driver to stop the car. We exited, and I stood near the gates, not so close I would alarm the guard, and I gazed at the other side. The tree-dotted terrain past the fence was, naturally, the same as where I stood in Irbid. The border guards looked the same; the quiet peace of Jordan's countryside shimmered in the distance as well.

But I knew that just a few miles farther, real destruction and devastation were occurring. Since the Arab Spring, when street protests by civilians escalated into civil war, the country's citizens had lived through a decade of brutal conflict and a protracted humanitarian crisis. I reflected: *a mere consequence of birth determines whether one set of people lives in peace or a few miles away in utter hell.*

As a result of Syria's internal conflict, millions of Syrians were forced to live without electricity, basic food items turned unaffordable, and fuel became a precious commodity. Millions migrated to Jordan, like the Iraqis a decade earlier. By 2022, "nine out of 10 Syrians are living in poverty and are unable to afford basic necessities such as bread, milk, and meat. The local currency devalued sharply over the years in parallel with the crash in neighboring Lebanon, and food prices spiked by more than a 100 percent. Nearly 7 million remain internally displaced and cash-strapped with no means to rebuild their homes and communities."[2]

I was reminded of Syria's deprivations months after standing at the gate, when I tried to replace Tunisian and Lebanese stocks in my portfolios with companies from surrounding countries. Syria was off limits. The country was listed on the US Department of Treasury's Office of Foreign Assets Control list, and investments in the country were illegal per US law. Though I saw opportunities to invest in rebuilding infrastructure, I was prohibited from allocating capital. Foreign investment might have reconnected grid lines, rebuilt homes and businesses, and enabled a suffering population to build wealth again.

While millions of Syrians lived in penury and desperation, the United States and Europe imposed sanctions, used both as a punitive measures against what was deemed a "world-leading state sponsor of terrorism" but also as diplomatic leverage to break through a persistent deadlock that has faced negotiations over Syria's future.

As local people craved access to capital to rebuild electric grids, run their enterprises, and rise above their deprivations, Western sanctions banned reconstruction of any sort, including reconstruction of power plants and pulverized cities. Once again, blind power stood in the way of prosperity for the people being ruled.

The Cost of Divestment

Sanctions are sometimes used in an attempt to peacefully change governmental policy in war-torn countries or to stop deadly attacks on civilians. This had been the US government's intention in imposing sanctions on Syria.

The lesson had been learned a world away decades prior. In the 1980s, investors banded together to demand that South Africa end its racist apartheid system. Following decades of oppression and brutality against the country's black majority, investors came to realize how their invested billions were unwittingly propping up the nation's status quo. A divestment program ensued, in which investors pulled their money out until change came. As a result, the end of that country's apartheid system was hastened.

Nobel Peace Prize winner Archbishop Desmond Tutu credited investors—more specifically, divestors—with helping to end the brutality. In 2010, he wrote, "In South Africa, we could not have achieved our freedom and just peace without the help of people around the world, who through the use of non-violent means, such as boycotts and divestment, encouraged their governments and other corporate actors to reverse decades-long support for the Apartheid regime."[3]

The role of capital in supporting governments, philosophies, and corporate actions had come to light. In the decades since, similar divestment strategies have become prominent. Most recently, Archbishop Tutu himself moved to leverage historical precedent to mitigate risk from another hostile source: climate change. In 2014, he pleaded, "Just as we argued in the 1980s that those who conducted business with apartheid South Africa were aiding and abetting an immoral system, we can say that nobody should profit from the rising temperatures, seas and human suffering caused by the burning of fossil fuels."[4]

But divestment strategies are often fraught with challenges. For example, some sustainable investors limit exposure to tobacco companies or fossil fuel companies in their investment portfolios, maintaining that they choose not to fund such "sin" companies. One challenge of this strategy is that investor definitions of "sin" stocks vary widely. Which humanitarian or planetary violations go too far, and, hauntingly, which are acceptable?

These moral dilemmas often have two sides. For example, some large investors in the United States prohibit investments in Israel because of their concerns about human rights violations against Palestinians. I experienced the hostility with my own eyes. From Jordan, I took a day trip over the Jordan River to visit Israel. As the guards loaded me and other travelers onto the buses, I noticed tanks deployed along the Israeli side, staring us down with large-caliber, high-velocity guns pointed mere feet from our bus—on both sides. I sat next to an older Palestinian man, and I had the feeling one false move could result in the bus being blown up.

After crossing the border, entering Israel was a snap for me. With my American passport and my mother's Jewish heritage, the questions by Israeli guards were simple and friendly. My co-passenger was next to me had to talk to another guard, and he wasn't so lucky. The guard berated him as he pleaded to enter. "Did you assist in the suicide bombing last week?" the guard demanded. My seatmate had tears in his eyes as he answered, "No, of course not." He dropped to his knees and begged, "Please. My son is dying. I need to see him in the West Bank Territories." After a tense exchange, the guard let him in.

While some investors may be unwilling to hold Israeli stocks, others are pouring in funds. This subjective assessment creates yet another challenge for divestment. For sanctions to work, they require scale. Sanctions (or divestment) theory suggests that if investors are unwilling to hold a stock, they will choke that country (company) from accessing the required capital to execute its objectives, thereby increasing its cost of capital. If those investors shun the stock, the price will fall from a lack of buyers, and the stock is deemed unattractive. However, at that lower price, unless there is wide agreement on the "sinful" nature of the holding, a value-oriented buyer likely awaits on the other side.

Without broad agreement, divestment in effect lowers the bar for agreeable investors to invest in "sin" countries' companies. Divestment's impact may be the opposite of what was intended. Here we see the onus of governance shift to the other side. What are the motives of the countries levying the sanctions?

Finally, is divestment delivering the intended solution? Over time, it exacerbates the challenge. As Syrians' lines of commerce and communication are cut short, their desperate cries for help are silenced. The impact of sanctions is in effect not the provision of aid but rather the continuance of prolonged misery.

The Syrian sanctions example extends to company-level divestment as well. In divesting companies that don't adhere to desired norms or practices, investors lose their opportunity to engage with these companies to actually effect change. Divestment displaces the investment from the table, cutting the opportunity for engagement and allowing alternative parties, perhaps with differing objectives, to redirect the company's aims.

A stunning recent example comes from the fossil fuel sector. In late 2020, the largest US energy company, ExxonMobil, found itself caught in a proxy battle with a tiny investor called Engine No 1. The investor had a miniscule stake in the company, owning only 0.02% of the company's total shares, but was able to use its stake to collaborate with other large shareholders and insist that the energy behemoth, long considered a climate change denier, take action on environmental risks. In a dramatic and unexpected turn at the company's annual shareholder meeting, Engine No 1 fought against the giant and won. The small investor shook up the company's governance structure and insisted on capital investments in novel carbon capture technology. Engine No 1 showcased that the power of capital in not divesting but rather investing.

Investing in Change

So what's a responsible investor to do?

The options at first appear stark: (1) to buy when there's "blood in the streets," risking that capital may be poured into the wallets of the rich, corrupt, and dangerous leaders, or (2) to withhold capital, restricting access to funds that create jobs, provide shelter, and feed families.

Today's megathemes, combining the power of capital with the rise of technology and sustainable finance, are reshaping the opportunity for this emerging part of the world. With technology, humans are more interconnected than ever, and more people's voices can be heard. Multiple nations can rise up as one, as we've seen in such movements as the Arab Spring.

Multiple issues helped spark the Arab Spring, including global warming, authoritarianism, food scarcity, systemic inequality, and rising prices. Technology fanned its flames, sending these sparks via social media across the Middle East, from Tunisia to Libya, Egypt, Yemen, Syria, and Bahrain.

Just as we are all connected, some of our most pressing concerns are as well. Climate change exacerbated suffering in the Middle East and triggered in part the Arab Spring movement. In a much-quoted chapter of a 2013 study by the Center for American Progress, the Center for Climate and Security, and the Stimson Center, Sarah Johnstone and Jeffrey Mazo note:

> ... in the distinct chain of events that led to the Arab Spring . . . [a] proximate factor behind the unrest was a spike in global food prices, which in turn was due in part to the extreme global weather in 2010–2011 ...This was not enough to trigger regime change—we have seen food-price spikes and food riots before—but it was a necessary part of this particular mix.[5]

As we look for effective tools to face these sustainability challenges, the megathemes also promise new solutions. For example, investment stewardship brings more players to the table in diplomatic solutions; as international companies become larger than countries, diplomacy evolves to include the private sector and private capital in dialogue. With more voices at the table, especially those with deeper pools of capital, direct engagement may prove a promising tool to advocate for humanitarian measures in Syria and beyond.

Technology's role in uniting citizens confers to investors as well. We are now able to not only engage jointly, but we can also invest jointly as well. The evolving field of blended finance enables private capital investors to co-invest with traditional concessionary capital. This format enables private investors to preserve their required return profiles, and it also enables the investors to achieve for the ultimate objective of the sustainability movement: measurable, positive impact.

The Long Road Out of the Ruins

Back in the days of ancient Rome, when Tunisia was known as Carthage, Hannibal, whom scholars regard as one of the greatest military minds in history, led North African elephants over the mountain passes through the Alps for one of the most spectacular surprise attacks ever recorded. My family visited the ancient city of Carthage, but there wasn't much to see anymore. Set before the shimmering blue of the Mediterranean, this crushed cityscape, with its husks of long-demolished buildings, looked primordial. Where the villas and theaters of Carthage once stood, only ghostly looking shapes remained, eroded by the passage of time. A solitary column stood in their midst, upright and alone.

Twenty years after Hannibal's death, the Romans defeated the Carthaginians, taking control of the entire Mediterranean basin. "*Delenda est Carthago!*" the orator Cato the Elder famously thundered in the Roman Senate. ("Carthage must be destroyed!") The city was plundered, then burned to the ground. Everything was decimated, including the manuscripts in its famous library. Nikhil and I briefed our sons on this dramatic story, then let them scamper through its famous archeological ruins.

"Except for Hannibal, Tunisia is not a country of fighters," a broker in Tunis joked with me a few days later. Proud though the history may be, he wanted to be clear they'd put the past behind them.

But have they really? While I had hoped that the events of the Arab Spring could be the turning point that enabled Tunisia to emerge, the horrifying events at the Bardo National Museum unfolded.

An emerging country lies in a balance of its own making. The power of capital lies in waiting; we want to invest in rough-and-tumble circumstances. If sustainable governance cannot prevail, however, which countries will be left behind in ruins?

6

Harnessing Domestic-Driven Demand

India's Unique Opportunity for Sustainable Growth

When the British declared India independent in 1947, the newly minted nation was left scrambling. The imperialists had colonized the subcontinent and instituted their restrictive customs over a rich culture that had developed for more than 6,000 years. When the British left, they divided the colony along the lines of religion: Muslim Pakistan and largely secular India. Many Muslims left India for Pakistan, but a majority of Sikhs and Hindus, like my father's family, fled from Pakistan to India. While 15 million displaced people were in transit, a million people in both groups were massacred.

My father often spoke of his joy growing up "in the ditches" of the refugee camps, but neither he nor my grandparents ever spoke about the journey there. Mobs attacked the trains of fleeing people, killing as many as they could. My father was on one of those so-called "blood trains," and to this day, I don't know how he made it through alive. His feelings toward tragedy were clear: *Don't look back; forgive and forget.*

The scars of that time were buried beneath the enormous bustle of the subcontinent's masses by the time I came to Lucknow as a pre-med student. I used to love wandering through the labyrinthine spaces above the main hall of Bara Imambara,[1] an ornate, massive meeting hall built by the Mughals, a Shia Muslim empire that was the last hold-out before Britain's East India Company finally swept their mantle over the entire country. Millions of Indians were made into indentured servants to serve the "company" and shipped overseas to pay off imaginary debts by working company holdings such as sugar plantations.[2] Bara Imambara tells a story of a pre-colonial opulence, with 1,000 interconnected passages hidden behind 500 near-identical pointed archways.

India today is a paradox. On the plus side, it is the largest and most vibrant democracy in the world. As of 2020, it was home to one-sixth of the world's population.[3] It is now on the brink of massive economic growth. Hundreds of millions who once lived in poverty are poised to enter the country's burgeoning middle class. Like China, India is on the edge of becoming a dominant world market. It will become a $5 trillion economy by 2024, making it the third-largest economy on earth, following the United States and China.

But India still faces enormous challenges, including an acute need for development, especially for the poorest of the poor. Because it's a democracy, the people are given a voice in how India progresses, but progress moves at the pace of trust. Because projects frequently incur discussion and debate, building trust takes time. In China, the government can undertake enormous infrastructure projects at will, usually with muted resistance from its citizens. Villages have been emptied, then submerged, in the name of development. With the creation of massive hydroelectric projects, such as Three Gorges Dam, for example, millions of Chinese citizens were uprooted before its completion in 2012. Some would say that it's a good thing that you can't do the same in India, but others point out how its progress is so slow, many people will die before they have the chance to be lifted out of poverty.

In agriculture, education, and industrialization, India has advanced rapidly. Unfortunately, this growth has led to an exceptionally wide gap between its rich and poor citizens. Perhaps nothing illustrates this more than Antilia, a private skyscraper in Mumbai, rising near the Arabian Sea, which billionaire Mukesh Ambani built as a residence for his family in 2012. In the shadows of this 27-floor, futuristic skyscraper is a shantytown of the desperately poor. Statistically speaking, one study found that roughly 65% of Mumbai's population lived in these shabby, rundown slums.[4]

On a separate issue, religious strife remains. I vividly remember a trip to the train station, heading from Lucknow to Mumbai, when an announcer broke through the music on the car radio to announce that bombs had been found on the train tracks. Minutes later, my driver pulled up to the majestic Charbagh Railway Station, built in the 1920s and world renowned for its soaring, fanciful towers. To my astonishment, it was business as usual. No one seemed to care about the threat. People were hurrying through the station's famous white arches, then along platforms to their trains.

When I reached the door to my train, I stopped. Was I really going to get on? Would I ignore the fact that more bombs could be lying in wait just because everyone else was? I took a deep breath and climbed aboard.

Such episodes of threatened violence—this constant strife—were ultimately caused by income inequality and the miserably low incomes and compromised educations of so much of the population. Now I had to figure out, *could a country with so many challenges really become a star in the world of emerging markets?*

Microfinance: The Original Impact Investing

After I gave up on being a frontier doctor, instead of returning home in defeat, I decided to change my course right there in India. I knew what my father would say if I told him I gave up on being a doctor: "I don't care what you do, Asha, just be the best." No pressure at all. If I didn't excel, I would only be tormented by that moment, gazing at poor families in a rural hospital.

At the time, I knew little about economics. I knew that India was staggering under the weight of its poverty, and I knew that money played a role. What if I worked that summer for a bank? In an Indian phone book, under B for "Bank," I found the Banker's Institute of Rural Development. No one answered the phone when I called, though. Undaunted, I hailed a rickshaw.

I arrived at a very small building outside the city, on a seemingly endless grassy plain under a bright blue sky. I was far from the city's

honking and blaring. I came upon the co-founder of the Banker's Institute in the courtyard, deep in meditative yoga. The rich, sensual scent
of his sandalwood incense welcomed me. On tiptoe I walked to the first
door I saw.

Seated at a table, brimming with masses of paperwork, was his wife.
I learned that they ran the Institute together, and they were happy to
have me come along and shadow them. I may have still been the crazy
American girl, but at least I had found someone who was glad to have me.

Soon they were taking me in a jeep down rural roads and then off the
roads, onto bumpy uncharted paths deep in the woods. Finally, we arrived
in a tiny rural village in the stifling heat. Mr. and Mrs. Vidyarthi spoke
to me in perfect English to set my expectations. "We are going there to
talk with them to improve their livelihoods," they told me. That was no
small goal.

We exited the vehicle, and I followed behind the couple, somewhat
embarrassed by my jeans, simple top, and frizzy, short hair. I could make
out a sea of colors within a group of several dozen women in bright saris,
and the occasional flash of a gold bracelet or chain caught my eye. More
than one woman wore a thin chain with a hanging charm of the Ashoka
wheel, the sign atop India's national flag.

As we approached the group, I remained silent, as I couldn't speak
their language.

The gathering was composed of about 30 women. Some were old,
with lined foreheads and large, yearning eyes that begged for compassion.
When their mouths opened wide, I could make out missing and black-
ened teeth. A few women had babies tied to their backs, eyes highlighted
with *kajal*, a charcoal eyeliner believed to ward off evil spirits, and some
were wide-eyed young girls.

As Mrs. Vidyarthi spoke in Hindi, the women listened with rapt attention. In the scorching heat, they wiped their brows with the ends
of their six-foot-long saris. Flies buzzed around us, and occasionally we
would swat them away.

Her husband translated for me. One woman declared that if she had
a cow, she could sell the milk. A teenage bride spoke up after her, saying
that if she had a sewing machine, she would be the most sought-after
seamstress in town. Listening to differing goals of the women, Mr. and
Mrs. Vidyarthi believed that they could help. Instead of loaning money
to them individually, they would ask the women of the village to band

together. That way, if one woman couldn't pay, the others in the group could pick up the deficit. Social pressures of the community would ensure that each would pay their owed amount.

I was hired as a volunteer. Because I could type, my summer job was to log the loans, dates, repayments, and the uses of the capital we provided. In this last column, my notes would list such items as "cow" and "sewing machine."

The concept of "microloans" is credited to Muhammad Yunus, a Bangladeshi economist who would later win the Nobel Peace Prize. Commercial banks shunned the poor because they were unable to provide collateral. Yunus realized that, lending just a few dollars per person, he could transform the poorest communities. Once people had pulled themselves up by starting new businesses, they could hire their neighbors and pay them for goods and services. Together, the community could ratchet itself up.

Visiting the villages, I soon learned of some of the drawbacks of microfinance lending. For example, one woman couldn't buy her farm supplies because she found her husband had taken the money and spent it on booze; another woman yelled at her group because, unlike them, she had paid off her loan, and now she had to pay for their poor decisions.

Yet I learned that microfinance worked when done right. This was when microfinance was recording great success in Bangladesh. Microfinance contributed to a steady rise in wealth in Bangladesh. One study showed that, within a 20-year period, extreme poverty decreased from 75% to 15% among long-term participants in a microfinance lending program, but only from 78% to 21% among nonparticipants.[5] The authors concluded that microfinance accounted for more than 10% of the total poverty alleviation.

Much of this success is attributed to Grameen Bank, founded by Yunus himself. Before Grameen Bank and microfinance, commercial banks shunned the poor because they were unable to provide collateral. Yunus' vision focused on the poorest of the poor. Specifically, he focused on women who were fed up with being excluded, like the ones that I met in India who stood under rain and in the sunshine dreaming out loud.

These loans mean more to a poor person, and they are taken seriously. The social structure keeps the borrowers accountable, a clever solution in a population where you can't run a credit check. At Grameen Bank, even though 80% of global borrowers earn less than $2 per day, they pay back their loans as much or at a higher rate than wealthier borrowers. Interestingly, Yunus also discovered women have better repayment rates than men.[6]

For me, this was exactly the evidence that I needed. The power of capital, put in the right hands, could make a real difference for a struggling community.

So many factors positioned India to succeed in microfinancing. For one, it has the largest rural population in the world. Since microfinancing is tailored to groups rather than individuals, a larger group is better able to cushion itself against shocks. Second, most of that large rural population could not obtain ordinary loans. Commercial banks were not interested in nickel-and-dime financing in remote pockets of the country.

At this time, in 1991, the nation had just launched its New Economic Policy (NEP), which opened its economy through such means as liberalization, privatization, and globalization.[7] The NEP made it easier for people to start a business, hence making paying off loans more possible. All these factors would contribute to the subsequent economic revolution in India.

Yet the "growth at any cost" model that the microfinance industry encouraged in India would become detrimental over time. For example, we worked with an inexperienced farmer who borrowed money for maize cultivation. In desperate need for high yield, she used harmful fertilizers that depleted the soil's nutrients. Although the farmer made her short-term profits, in the long term she will lose all her gains as her yield plummets. In addition, her community suffers from harmful land and water pollution.

Investors and stakeholders, like me, began recognizing the responsibility of investors in generating a more sustainable world that can deliver both financial and social returns. A few years later, the acronym ESG was coined. The founding executive director, James Gifford, once told me that he at first thought to name the strategy just plain ES—for environmental and social. The G, for governance, came along later: "I added the G at the end of ES to give it some heft."

Like the Ashoka wheel on the Indian flag, in which dozens of principles come together to form one spinning wheel, ESG investing emphasizes a systems-based perspective. As investors become aware of how investments interact with the broader ecosystem, we see that all parts of our ecosystem—external environment, social communities, and internal governance—must come together to inform every investment decision. ESG investing calls on investors to recognize how integrated we are.

Responsible Investing Is Born

The enormous ballroom was awash with color, from the fuchsia flower arrangements on gold-accented tables to the kaleidoscopic colors of the saris worn by the female guests. The setting, though, was midtown Manhattan. The guests included business leaders from across the globe. The occasion was a 2005 dinner given by the Indian consulate in honor of the Prime Minister of India, Dr. Manmohan Singh, there to address the sixtieth United Nations General Assembly.

Dr. Singh, an Oxford-trained economist, had long been one of my heroes. In the early 1990s, when the country was on the verge of economic collapse, Dr. Singh, then the finance minister, initiated various reforms, ranging from encouraging foreign investments in India to privatizing state-run industries. These actions ushered in an era of high economic growth for India. I was also drawn to Dr. Singh for his immigration story, which resembled my father's. He, too, had arrived in India after being forced, under Partition, to leave the part of India that would become Pakistan.

Seated next to me were legendary business leaders, including two of the four famous Hinduja brothers—all billionaires—who run a century-old Anglo-Indian transnational conglomerate called the Hinduja Group. Known for his distinct sartorial style, S. P. Hinduja's pink silk tie was as bright as any sari in the room.

Even as the vegetable biryani and paneer makhani was served, the conversation scarcely flagged. We all talked animatedly through the evening. The Hindujas, too, had experienced the horrors of Partition. New stories that I hadn't heard before came out; I was moved to hear my father and S. P. Hinduja reference their post-Partition lives. Then it hit me. Here I was among a group of Indians, many of whom, like my own father, had grown up in the direst poverty. Yet now they were being sumptuously fêted in one of the great capitals of the world.

It was an honor to talk to these Indians who had climbed to such heights, and I imagined that more Indians would have the same chance. But the nation faces ingrained challenges of culture that may not be so easily overcome.

During vacations as a child, I was exposed to some of the economic disparities in India. I would stay with well-off family members who lived in mansions staffed by armies of servants. I would catch glimpses of these silent figures as they moved unobtrusively through the household, like shadows. At night they slept on hard wooden floors in their employers' homes. They were all but invisible.

During one of our visits, I watched a young servant as she gracefully moved from one task to the next. She was six or seven years old, I thought at the time. I now realize that she was likely older: malnutrition has a way of making people look younger. Even as young as I was, I sensed that something was very wrong here. *Where are her parents?* I wondered. *Why isn't she with her playmates?*

Though officially the caste system was ended in 1950, these servants were invariably from the "untouchable"[8] caste, so low that it was thought unclean to touch them. When I imagined what my life might be like had I grown up in India, I usually pictured myself like the owners of the mansions. But what if I had been born an untouchable?

The effect of India's caste system is that the poor remain poor and even get poorer. Furthermore, because whole segments of the Indian population are excluded from making the most of their economic potential, the caste system carries significant economic costs in India. Barack Obama succinctly states in *Promised Land*, "despite its genuine economic progress, though, India remained a chaotic and impoverished place: largely divided by religion and caste, captive to the whims of corrupt local officials and power brokers, hamstrung by a parochial bureaucracy that was resistant to change."

Corruption is another major issue in India. In 2009, 13,000 supposed employees of a profitable Indian tech company were revealed to have never existed. All of them were being paid a regular wage, totaling around $3 million a month.[9] The year before, the same company, Satyam, was the winner of the "Golden Peacock" for corporate governance, a national award highlighting their compliance and risk management. Now the owners had to explain an enormous case of missing persons.

What became known as the Satyam scandal rocked the world of Indian finance and produced larger questions about practices across the country. When he saw a goldmine to be made in local real estate, the owner, B. Ramalinga Raju, had cooked up an excuse to buy thousands of acres of land with company money. He thought for sure he'd be able to turn a profit, but every time he tried to close the gap it became wider. According to the *Hindustan Times*, Raju said, "It was like riding a tiger, not knowing how to get off without being eaten."

The company, run by Raju and two of his brothers, was revealed to be falsifying invoices and tax documents and lying to shareholders. Their stock dropped from the previous year's high of 544 rupees to less than 12 rupees in January 2009. Raju, his brothers, and seven others were all convicted and given seven years in prison.

Some commentators speculated that one cause of the scandal was systemic. Corruption is inherent in a culture that promotes people based on their caste and gender rather than their qualifications.[10] Just as members of the lowest castes are still servants, many businesses still want to give their highest posts to people who fit a certain rubric: male, not Muslim, and a member of the highest castes. The name Raju is a variant of "Raja"; Satyam was run by men from a royal caste.

Investors can prioritize finding new methods to solve old systemic issues. Here, the ESG model has proven valuable. The G (governance) in ESG, also referred to as responsible investing, has the potential to boost economic growth by encouraging transparency and ethical practices, while promoting investor confidence. It is positioned to expose lurid examples of poor governance like the Satyam scandal.

Just across the Charles River from my office in Boston, George Serafeim, a young, brainy, little-known professor at the Harvard Business School was doing pioneering work that addressed these types of questions. Serafeim's research showed how responsible investments added value to portfolios. He'd also taken the process a step further, showing that the responsible investment practices that companies adopted needed to be "material" to the company's success.

By coining the term *materiality*, Serafeim set off a movement. On a frigid winter day, I found myself sitting on a tawny brown leather couch in Serafeim's cozy office, sharing a data dilemma with him. I wanted his thoughts on how to cover indicators from the inefficient, illiquid markets that I followed most closely.

"How were you able to get this level of detail from companies?" I asked incredulously as I scanned the data he'd received, which included customer privacy policies and details on energy management approaches and gender diversity.

His answer was disarmingly simple: "I wrote to companies directly and asked them to sign NDAs [nondisclosure agreements]." How clever, I thought, but I can't do that for my 40,000 stock universe.

With the work done by Gifford, who first coined responsible investing, and by Serafeim with his materiality research, I brought my investment firm to shore its commitment. We became the first systematic investor to sign the UN Principles of Responsible Investment (UN-PRI), a UN-supported network of investors that incorporate responsible investing in their investments, and other tirelessly working investors. We were assuring our commitment that E, S, and G in ESG *all* mattered in creating long-term value for companies.

As investors, we need to build portfolios that are "future fit"—that is, agile, adaptive, nimble, responsive, and resilient to our changing world. We must recognize the power of our capital. By leveraging it to build structures that are intentionally stable and regenerative, we reinforce its value. India, in particular, is positioned to gain for responsible investments that have the potential to decrease risk factors rising from national challenges. Analysts show that the governance policies will have the largest impact on share prices in India because of the poor governance that presently exists.

Clear Skies Behind the Smog

The weather in Delhi was sweltering, and I was tired. My father and I were visiting his mother in Bhiwani, and with a long drive ahead, I lay down in the backseat of the tan Maruti Suzuki. When we arrived, I climbed the pastel-colored steps to her home. Yet after I had walked only a few steps, I collapsed.

In the hospital they told me the rest of what happened. I lapsed into a dehydration-induced coma caused by the extreme heat, receiving a gash on my head from my fall. My mother says she nearly died that day when she learned I was in a coma half a world away.

My father found a needle and thread from his older sister's sewing kit, dipped the needle and the thread in alcohol, and proceeded to sew the cut without anesthesia. All this because the local hospital was out of sterile stitches. When my father passed me the mirror the next day, I smiled wryly at the thick black, fraying thread that was stitched just above my nose.

As climate change worsens, researchers speculate that India will be a major victim of more frequent and intense heat waves. One projection shows that, by 2030, this type of heat wave could afflict two hundred million people in India alone, leading to more heat-related illnesses and impacting economic growth.[11]

Drought is a frequent issue in the hot climate, and the situation could get worse for Indian farmers. In early 2021 widespread protests broke out among Indian farmers because new laws threatened to cut protection for farmers as the government transitioned to privatizing the agricultural sector. One factor in the farmers' fears was that the number of extreme climate events has tripled in their lifetimes and threaten their livelihood.[12]

Litter is another scourge. It's everywhere on the subcontinent, especially the ubiquitous plastic bags favored by Indian shoppers. These come in cotton candy colors, rather like the pastel-hued saris favored by so many Indian women. Cheery or not, these discarded bags are an ecological nightmare.

The deadly heat waves, droughts, and polluted rivers take a heavy toll on the livelihood of Indians, especially in the agriculture sector. Since agriculture contributes the most to the India economy (approximately 60% of the Indian population works in the industry, contributing about 18% to India's GDP),[13] climate change would mean more bad news for India's troubled economy.

Second, the country's poorest are the worst hit by the effects of climate change. Not only do they suffer the most from the food insecurity that arises from a dwindling agriculture sector, but also they are more susceptible to the effects of heat waves, droughts, and unclean water.

Here too, age-old traditions are causing ill effects in the modern era. True believers will tell you that a single dip in the holy waters of the Ganges will wash away 100 lifetimes of bad karma. At my baby brother's *mundan*—the Hindu ritual in which a male infant's head is shaved, then washed in the Ganges—it was hot, earthy, and otherworldly all at once. I was fascinated that baptisms could occur in the same water in which cows defecated and cremated bodies were dumped. Sewage flowed past the front door of my grandparents' house in Bhiwani into the same river, and I never got used to the sight of squatting Indian men, their trousers bunched around their ankles as they defecated by the riverbanks.

The Indian government recognizes that some of its pollution comes from the fossil fuels that choke the large cities, but India's greatest challenges are caused by the climate itself. The need for a framework to mitigate climate risk has become imperative.

At the Paris Agreement in 2015, Prime Minister Narendra Modi made India one of the first signatories. In an impassioned plea to other world leaders urging them to sign the agreement, Modi sagely linked climate change to human health. He spoke of how diseases can develop when industrializing zones encroach upon rural wildlife and how easily infections can travel in crowded, unsanitary environments. While Modi was referring to such illnesses as malaria and dengue, his words could have been applied to COVID-19.

Modi's pro-growth agenda for India included building hundreds of millions of clean toilets around the country and cleaning up rivers of filth, bold commitments to the global community of environmental protections. These included planning a net-zero-emissions rail network by 2030; developing a National Clean Air Programme, focusing on air-quality management for 102 cities; and banning single-use plastics in the mega city of Mumbai. Modi made these commitments in recognition of the impact of climate on India's social stability and economic vitality

Within a year of the Paris Agreement, I launched the world's first actively managed emerging markets fossil-fuel-free investment strategy.[14] This portfolio shifted investments out of the energy and materials sectors and into high-growth consumer ones; it also shifted exposures from more corrupt emerging markets in favor of more stable, better-governed ones, and it demonstrated that a sustainable solution doesn't have to come at a cost.

For India, as for other countries, the transition to a low-carbon economy presents new possibilities. These include emerging sectors like clean technologies and renewable solutions. I saw this change when I boarded an electric rickshaw in 2019. Who would have thought that the nearly two million auto rickshaws and buses that coughed carbon dioxide in all the Indian cities would be fitted with electric motors that are on India's roads today—more than the total number of electric cars sold in the United States?[15]

In addition, a low-carbon economy presents an opportunity for the poor to leap forward with new technology. One example is the story of a young Indian man who grew up in a village in Lohardaga, deep in the heart of one of India's least developed areas. After 21 years of driving a bicycle rickshaw, earning about $2.50 a day, he rented an electric rickshaw to see if what he heard was true. By working faster, he could take on more jobs. Not only did he increase his take-home pay to about $7 a day, but the work was far less strenuous on his body than his old job.[16]

These scenarios represent the material investment opportunity for a low-carbon economy in India. Just as India is the third largest pollution emitter in the world, after the United States and China, it follows these nations as the third largest investor in renewable energy investments. The investment opportunity alone could contribute $218 billion per year to the Indian economy by 2030.[17]

In India, pollution is omnipresent, as are the negative health implications for its inhabitants. Yet the early stages of the pandemic contained a harbinger of the future. With the severe reduction in traffic, the notoriously yellowish skies of Delhi and other large Indian cities magically cleared. In the middle of my father's native state of Punjab, residents in the city of Jullundur were treated to a rare sight: a shimmering view of the Himalayas, visible from 100 miles away. It was like a window into a better, possible future.

SDG Integration and the Role of Technology

After leaving their family farm behind and living without water or electricity in the refugee camp, my grandparents were finally offered reparations by the government as a result of the land confiscation that had occurred years before in Pakistan. The home was a squat, two-story concrete structure in the isolated desert village of Bhiwani, 120 kilometers west of Delhi.

They still had no running water. Electricity came 10 years later and was intermittent. As in so many parts of India, rolling blackouts were the norm. I would visit my grandparents there in the summers, and on the surface, the town changed little from one visit to the next. But small differences added up.

One year, as we were driving from the airport, I was startled to see that the road, once rutted and unpaved, now gleamed with asphalt. There wasn't a pothole in sight. Manicured grass borders lined the road, along with rows of bright flowers. My astonishment grew as we passed a beauti-fully sculpted 20-foot-tall asphalt sign that read, "Welcome to Bhiwani."

As in so many emerging nations, this was a time when market liber-alization was driving change. While market mechanisms have their draw-backs, liberalized markets are very efficient ways to inject money into an economy, not to the government at the top but widely across the middle. Amid a campaign for rural development across the nation, Bhiwani had become a city.

Walking down the street, I experienced a sensory overload of a new sort. True, the pungent smells of turmeric and other pungent spices still mixed with the dung of the cows wandering the streets and such fragrant flowers as marigolds, jasmine, and roses. The streets were a blur of sound and motion. Street vendors called out; cars honked. Wild monkeys scur-ried along, and cows wandered the streets.

But tall buildings were rising up all around. At a local bank, customers' eyes were being scanned to verify their IDs before they could enter. In my aunt's living room hung the same tiny, primitive fan, but these days it runs all the time. Rolling blackouts are a thing of the past. Similarly, while the house's rickety sink and squat toilet remained unchanged, they now mainly work, thanks to the miracle of reliable plumbing.

The changes I witnessed in Bhiwani have, for the past few decades, been replicated across India. They have been driven by a combination of government capital, development funding, philanthropy, and private money. Since its launch of an aggressive privatization program in the 1990s, India has been one of the most progressive countries in driv-ing public–private partnerships, in which private investors join ones in the public sector to achieve progress. Private investors are drawn to these investments, not just out of a desire to lift up the poor but to generate returns. In particular, healthcare, which was poor and unreliable in the 1960s and 1970s, is now readily available and of such a high quality that people from around the world travel to India on "medical tourism."

In addition, India's education policies have had a meaningful role in promoting the lives of women. Today, they head five of the eleven larg-est banks in the country. And why not? Microfinance investments dec-ades ago raised the poorest of poor women in villages—teaching them to bank, make loans, save, and spend. Today, in stark contrast, the finance minister of this vibrant and chaotic country is a woman, Nirmala Si-tharaman, who was ranked by *Forbes* as thirty-fourth among the 100 most powerful women in the world in 2019.[18]

The prosperity of Indians and Indians abroad is a direct result of investments that founded world-class centers of education like the Indian Institutes of Technology, Indian Institutes of Management, and hundreds of medical schools. The latter send many highly qualified physicians to the United States, where Indian Americans today constitute almost 20% of all medical doctors. Engineers who graduated from the Indian Institutes of Technology run Microsoft, Alphabet, IBM, Twitter, and Adobe.

Technology has assisted not only those at the top. Throughout my travels I have noticed that tech has been intertwined with all sorts of other changes. From clean technology to mobile technology, automation, and artificial intelligence, India uses technology-enabled solutions that are today sustainable and affordable.

On the whole, India has shown unparalleled technology growth. According to the Global Innovation Index, a score of a nation's innovation culture, India's ranking improved from 81 to 46 between 2015 and 2021, out of 132 nations.[19] In 2019, India also ranked third in the world in terms of attracting investment for technology transactions.[20] This prolific growth is often ascribed to the domestic talent (India produces some of the world's best coders and computer scientists), local entrepreneurs, and local investors who built an attractive tech ecosystem and also a market that has become more open to global investors.

Several of these innovations are geared toward achieving the Sustainable Development Goals (SDGs), a universal set of 17 objectives designed to meet urgent environmental, political, and economic challenges facing our world. These goals target specific global challenges, such as poverty, inequality, climate change, and environmental degradation. Essentially, SDGs were created as a framework to achieve the ESGs.

The SDGs supersede the UN Millennium Development Goals (MDGs), which were set up to reduce poverty in developing nations. However, even though the MDGs recorded great success—such as lifting millions out of poverty—they had a narrow focus. The SDGs, on the other hand, provide a holistic approach that embed environmental, economic, and social aspects together.[21] The difference in impact becomes apparent in stories like the one in Bangladesh.

In April 2013, a grisly report came on the television news. A garment factory in Dhaka, the country's capital, had collapsed, crushing hundreds of workers, mostly women. The footage was horrifying—stunned, sobbing family members arriving at the scene; broken-looking bodies, some wrapped in bright saris; the sirens of countless emergency vehicles. I suspected that the factory owners had chosen not to sign a pact that would have required basic inspections for fire and electrical safety. But it wasn't only true about Bangladesh; I'd seen other companies in India make this same, unconscionable choice.

When companies implement SDGs into their business, cases like this are less prevalent because of an increased focus on both the economic and social impacts, such as protection of anyone involved in the making of products or provision of services. Those hundreds of women could still be alive if the garment company had adhered to basic labor-standards requirements.

Transforming Wonderland

Change has come slowly in this ancient, democratic land. Back in my pre-med days, I had wanted to launch a medical study, but first I had to get approval from King George's Medical College hospital. From the moment I passed through the hospital's elegantly arched doorways, it was like I was back in the labyrinth of Bara Imambara.

To be approved for the study, I had to chase down "the Principal's signature." I trafficked through the maze-like facility, paperwork in hand, being redirected from one bureaucrat to another: "The Principal is out today," "The Principal's deputy can sign." I was even asked, "Which Principal in fact?" as I chased the approval from one office to another among the winding warrens where the facility directors worked. Each meeting ended with complicated instructions leading me to the office where I was expected next. I felt like Alice in Wonderland, racing through one endless-seeming corridor after another, desperate for my crinkled paper to be signed.

Throughout the decades, government has recognized that bureaucracy stalls and frustrates progress.

But digitizing the paper has the power to unlock India. Recent years have demonstrated this power through the world-leading Aadhaar program, the world's largest biometric ID program. Instituted over the last decade, Aadhaar has created identities for the population, including the poorest and most marginalized. The "ID revolution" enabled every citizen to access the financial economy, to be brought into the formal economy, and to eschew the dreaded—at times even comical—layers of bureaucracy.

India's strong government has delivered transformative change not only through technology. Incredibly, the Modi government has mandated the electrification of the entire country – each slum, each city, and each village. It is hard to imagine an India without blackouts.

The government has wielded government capital to drive social change as well. With masses of Indian adults who still cannot read or write, disproportionately women, government has upended the government funding strategy for girls. While education was previously required for girls through grade 5, updated mandates (and associated funding) now set education compulsory for girls up to the tenth grade.

As such, things are changing especially quickly among the youth. The picture of an Indian girl, drawing a crowd of her parents, older uncles, and aunts as she teaches them how to search for Internet sites comes to mind. The youthful population (the largest in the world) are endowed with not only tech literacy, but traditional literacy rates have improved dramatically as well. Literacy among the youth has shown remarkable progress, as youth literacy contrasts dramatically with elder literacy.

Despite technology's promise in India, more investment and infrastructure are needed among the poorest populations. While the government has brought transformation to the country, much need remains. Rising temperatures scorch the land, sweltering and overcrowded cities are at risk of becoming uninhabitable, inequality exceeds its emerging market peers, and nearly 10% of the vast population still live in extreme poverty.

The conditions are ideal for the private sector to wield the power of capital to leverage the treasures on which India sits today: technology that eschews the British legacy of bureaucracy; a young, literate, and democratic populace; and the prowess of the third largest economy in the world. The opportunity is ripe for the country's business leaders to create jobs, foster innovation, and develop lasting, leading solutions for the country's citizens—and the globe's.

7

Data Is the New Oil

Africa Needs (Venture Funding), China Feeds (Seed Capital)

"Spain is not Uganda."

It was the text message read around the world. Back in 2012, Spanish Prime Minister Mariano Rajoy tapped out a note to his finance minister, who was then in the midst of negotiating $125 billion of new debt from the Eurozone to bail out Spain's banks.

"Stand your ground, we're the number four power in Europe," he typed, before adding, fatally: "Spain is not Uganda."

What was intended as a factual remark instead unleashed a storm of protest, in Africa and beyond. The hash tag #ugandaisnotspain ricocheted around the world, trending on Twitter and other social media.

After a certain amount of deft apologizing, Spain got the bailout agreement. Still, the comparison between the two countries begs several questions. Whose economy would we rather be invested in? Spain's population is wealthier than that of Uganda, but it doesn't necessarily reflect the future. Wealth is a backward-looking measure; it tells us the past history of Uganda's economy. Forward-looking measures tell us what might lay ahead, and those measures—like growth and productivity—are compelling for this East African nation.

When the headlines went global, I had just returned from a trip to Africa. I had witnessed one transition from old to new during a stay in

Botswana, just north of South Africa. In the taxi from the airport to the
capital city, Gaborone, we passed a nondescript warehouse. My driver
gleefully pointed out that it was full of diamonds, all neatly sorted and
shelved. This ordinary-looking building, he told me, held half of this nation's GDP.

A dependency on commodities in Africa was nothing new, but
something else was. Botswana was executing a transformational strategy:
to move up the value chain to emphasize skill development for its people and higher-value services to drive its economy. In 2013, DeBeers, the
world's leading diamond company, moved its refining operations from
London to Gaborone, creating hundreds of local jobs in the process. In
addition, DeBeers moved higher value-added jobs, like logistics and diamond distribution. Botswana was taking jobs from London.

More than a decade ago, when the text went viral, Africa was set
to be one of the highest growth regions across the emerging markets.
I highlighted the region as "where the BRICs [Brazil, Russia, India,
China] go for BRIC-like growth." The country was growing rapidly
with its large population, and foreign direct investment was pouring
in. While the investments were targeting the continent's commodity-
rich landscape, foreign investors were building out its backbone: roads,
seaports, airports, and other vital infrastructure, networking the continent with the potential to unleash a powerful, large, and underestimated
economy. A decade has passed, and infrastructure development continues
and evolves.

Today, the connectivity and infrastructure is less about roads and
ports, and more about telecom lines, satellites, Internet browsers, and 5G.

Africa is well positioned to leapfrog in the adoption of these technologies, given both its youth-fueled appetite for technology as well as
its social development needs. But as technology is financed and distributed alongside international partners, what will the consequences be?

East Africa's Silicon Savannah

On one sweaty *matatu* (minibus) ride from Mombasa to Nairobi in
Kenya, I was sandwiched between two women, whose wide hips and
buttocks left me with only a meager portion of my seat. They spoke
with me like I was an old friend, sharing stories of bargains that they

had made at the market. When Kimeli, a single mother and successful businesswoman, boasted about pricing a bag of rice down from KSh 136 to Ksh 124, they reached over me and slapped both palms together. I admired their spirit and energy, trying to understand more about how money filtered through their lives.

Days later, while in Kenya's Westgate Mall with my family, I received the worrying news of a bombing at the Mombasa bus stop. I couldn't stop thinking of those two women. *Were they safe at home with their children, whom they spoke so lovingly of? Could they have been at the bus station that day?* Ironically, a few months prior, 71 shoppers at the Westgate mall had also been gunned down by extremists. As I stood in front of the crowded Adidas store with my young son tugging at my shirttails while pointing at fancy shoes, I swallowed the giant lump in my throat.

I also wondered about those extremists. *Why did they do it? Were they impoverished and undereducated?* The history of Kenya is rich with ethnic strife, tribes combatting one another after generations of tension. *Could economic development and broad financial inclusion relieve this tension?* I wondered.

The next day, as I took a taxi to my first business meeting of the trip, my mind similarly mulled over the dozens of questions I wanted to ask, this time directed toward the management team of Safaricom, one of the largest telecommunication networks in sub-Saharan Africa (SSA) and the preeminent leader in the mobile-money movement. I was distracted by a persistent teenage street vendor who had taken advantage of the slow traffic to brandish perfectly sliced oranges at my window.

"I have no cash," I said, rolling down my window. This was my attempt to send him to a more interested customer.

"No problem. You do phone transfer," he responded with a wide smile.

Twenty minutes later, I was standing outside the Safaricom House with three oranges tucked into my briefcase.

Sometimes a moment comes along when the world slows down, and we're afforded the opportunity to reflect in real time. Standing in front of the Safaricom office building, I remembered a day in 2007, the year I formally started covering frontier markets. That day Safaricom had raised nearly $1 billion from its initial public offering. I remember my raised heart rate and the goosebumps on my arms from the hope I felt.

In retrospect, I could never have anticipated how pivotal Safaricom would be, not for Kenya alone but for SSA as a whole. Safaricom has lifted several million Kenyan households out of poverty, especially in women-led households. It has created financial inclusion, which the World Bank says is a major way in which an emerging market can "leapfrog" the developed world. Finally, it has inspired spin-offs and competition such as M'Shwari—a saving and credit card service—and Orange Money in Ivory Coast that will continue to put Africa on the path to achieving sustainable development goals.

Once seated in a conference room in the Safaricom House, I reached for a pen in my purse, and my fingers grazed my bag's sliced oranges, now soggy from the heat. I knew I would not be eating them, as I had recently recovered from a stomach ailment in Lusaka, Zambia. I smiled, mirroring the mischievous smile from the teenage hawker.

He was a reminder of the far-reaching effect of Safaricom, specifically its mobile-money subsidiary: M-Pesa. If the same scenario were repeated just a few years ago, the business-minded orange seller would have had to take my excuse of having no cash and pursue another customer. Now, unless I claimed to not have a phone, then pleading no money was a silly excuse.

M-Pesa was founded by a team that recognized the need for Kenyans to exchange money. Despite an abundance of banks, people were unbanked. Many worked in informal unemployment and needed easy ways to be paid. Others were literally putting cash on a bus and sending it to family, hoping it would not be stolen.

Even with these obvious needs, the founders did not anticipate M-Pesa's growth. M-Pesa has unarguably become the world's most successful mobile-money platform. Its 49 million registered users conduct up to US$15 billion in yearly transactions, such as paying utility bills, school fees, and salaries.[1] Case studies, from academia to development agencies, have been written about the profound success of this company—a striking example of how private sector development, market returns, and social advancements can all be made in synchrony with one another.

The company has grown a network of nearly a million agents, a stark contrast to the only 2,365 ATMs[2] in the country and a clear marker of M-Pesa's success in including customers better than the traditional banks. Statistically speaking, before M-Pesa, 26% of the population had access to financial transactions. As of 2018, that number was 75%.[3]

In addition, M-Pesa has reduced the cost of sending money internationally. For several Kenyans, sending money internationally via traditional banking stations has always been a costly and tedious affair, with long-hours spent in snaking lines. I once stood in one of those lines as a fight broke out. The cause was a young man mistakenly stepping on a person's foot, but in truth, those two people were tired and frustrated.

In 2008, two years after M-Pesa entered the market, the cost of sending US$100 domestically was about US$6 by postal money order and US$2 by the Western Union; these two were totally disrupted by the US$1 charge by M-Pesa.[4] On top of that, it offered instantaneous transfer.

At the Safaricom House, as I looked up from my notes halfway through our meeting, I noticed something else. I was one of only three females in a room of close to 30 people. This was not unusual for me as a female investor in finance. This time, though, I realized a new perspective dawning in this country.

I began to think of how transformative M-Pesa must be to female entrepreneurs and women-led homes. Let's use Kimeli, the vibrant single mother that I met at the Mombasa bus station, as an example. She sells rice at the Murthuwa market, and she is known for her adept bargaining skills. "If you want to get it cheap, tell Kimeli to buy it for you," her friend had told me. At the beginning of the day, Kimeli uses an M-Pesa loan to buy rice from a wholesale distributor.

Being a successful businesswoman, her stall is almost empty by the end of the day. She repays her loan and returns home with an M-Pesa account credited with enough money to pay her children's school fees. In the morning, she gets the kids ready for school, and before they leave the house, she transfers via M-Pesa their school fees to the school's account. They all get on the *Boda-Boda*; one child is lodged between her and the motorcycle driver, while the other child sits in front of the driver. When they arrive at her kids' school, she pays the driver using M-Pesa and heads toward the bus station to have another successful day at the market. M-Pesa provides Kimeli with a convenient way to provide for her family.

"How is AI impacting M-Pesa's current success?" I asked the meeting facilitator.

This question had burned in my mind throughout my taxi ride. I knew M-Pesa was a key player in the Silicon Savannah—a reference combining the tech scene of Silicon Valley and the grassland savanna ecosystem in Kenya. What I didn't know was whether the industry was poised to utilize artificial intelligence as it was in developed countries.

They were making strides. As the facilitator explained, every day, as 20 million users make payments and transfers, M'Shwari mobile credit services (through M-Pesa) uses built-in AI technology to collect metadata on the types of transactions in which a person engages. This shows how much money a person has and whether they have to capability to pay back the loan. That allows the AI to generate a credit score for each user. This has two benefits over the traditional method. First, it uses the most relevant inputs, so it's more accurate. Second, even the "unbanked" can get a credit score.

I could think of one other way in which AI applications could be used. I figured that M-Pesa penetration in Kenya is high and many people still have to key in dozens of digits to make a single payment. I drew from my own experience in quantitative methods to figure out this process could be simplified.

I could not have imagined then how AI would later be used to upgrade from the unstructured text interface system to a more seamless system like QR (quick response) codes.[5] QR codes have manifold benefits, and one of the most important is that they can be used for everything. You can use them to hold data, share Wi-Fi, engage in e-learning, and so much more. By integrating such a ubiquitous technology as QR codes, M-Pesa would later spread to several other regions and markets.

The meeting ended with congratulatory handshakes, laughter, and hope-filled conversations. As I walked outside, I pulled the bag of oranges from my bag, remembering in admiration how the teenager had teased me, "One will not be enough, Aunty. You need to buy plenty." Then I waited in eager anticipation for my cab. I would be spending the rest of my afternoon witnessing another exciting sector of technological innovation in the country. I looked forward to riding through the largest volcanic split in the crust of the earth: the Great Rift Valley.

Powered Up in South Africa

As my tour group approached the Hell's Gate National Park of the African Great Rift Valley located just outside Nairobi, I took in the astounding view. Within minutes, I was gushing over the giraffes, lions, zebras, and elephants roaming on the open savannah dotted with mountains, valleys, vegetation, and large lakes. Thousands of pink flamingos floated gracefully over the lakes, feasting on its rich algae. Gusts of steam shot skyward from the earth.

Rift Valley is nicknamed "the cradle of humanity" for our species' origins there because of its unique ability to support a wide diversity of life. Looking toward Kenya's future, it is also a fountain of immense heat emanating from within the earth's core. Scientists explain that as the tectonic plates underneath move, they cause breaks in the earth's crust that allow underground water to interact with superheated rock, turning it into steam. The steam gives Hell's Gate National Park its name.

The steam is directed through miles of tubes to the Olkaria Geothermal Plant, also within the park, and into turbines, generating clean energy that won't run out for millions of years. In total, the Olkaria plant generates 42% of Kenya's power,[6] making the country one of the 10 largest producers of geothermal energy in the world.[7]

Kenya is using that geothermal energy to increase its electrification rates. The benefits of this renewable energy over other sources, like solar or wind energy, is that it is not affected by climatic conditions. It is available all-day, all-year-round. Unlike natural gas, it is sustainable. As of 2020, it already helped provide 75% of Kenyans with access to electricity, a significant increase from 56% in 2016.[8]

That evening I got back to my hotel feeling optimistic. The renewable technology revolution was alive and well in SSA. But I was jolted back into reality when all the lights went out. As the whirring of the generator blended with the nocturnal sounds of nature, I was reminded that more than two out of three people in SSA still had no access to electricity. I couldn't help but think of all the people who could not afford backup electricity generators: children with no lights to study and hence break free from the cycle of poverty; the adults holding onto phones with dead batteries, unable to access their banking apps; and all the local hospitals unable to perform emergency surgeries.

I began to think that electricity was the key Africa needed to unlock prosperity. *If everyone had access to electricity, there would be much less poverty and much more equality.* Yet that was only a piece of the puzzle, as my experiences at the southern tip of the continent had shown.

South Africa is an outlier compared with the rest of SSA. While the average electricity access rate for the SSA region is 47% (78% in the urban areas and 28% in the rural areas), South Africa has an overall access rate of 85%.[9] Despite the fact, however, that it is almost equally distributed between the rural and urban areas, the country still has the highest income inequality in the world.[10] More than half of the population lives below the national poverty line.[11]

Visiting South Africa, I could see the inequality with my naked eye. The rich enjoy the numerous benefits of electricity. Their appliances are powered throughout the day, enabling them to connect with the digital world 24/7. Meals are cooked on electric stoves, saving them from the harmful smoke of alternatives such as firewood. They take time-saving appliances like dishwashers and washing machines for granted. For the millions of South Africans living below poverty line, the story is vastly different.

When I entered a taxi in Johannesburg, I was greeted by an oily smell. It reminded me of my paternal grandmother's kitchen in India, where most meals were cooked over a kerosene stove.

After a few minutes, Loyiso, my taxi driver, took on the role of a tour guide. Among other sights he showed me the statues of Nelson Mandela and Desmond Tutu. Their efforts had in some ways laid the foundation for sustainability investing. During my undergraduate years at Stanford, I came to learn of the work—motivated by Nelson Mandela—that advocated for divesting South African assets from foreign investment strategies. If global investors withheld capital from the region, the philosophy went, South African leaders would be forced to take action to end apartheid. The sustainability movement in its earliest days learned pointers from this strategy. In the years since, popular sustainable strategies have included anti-tobacco and fossil-fuel–free campaigns.

"Do you know this place?" he asked, smiling broadly, and pointing at the headquarters for Eskom. I wasn't expecting that.

"Eskom," I said, "the electricity company?"

South Africa's public electricity company derived its electricity predominantly from coal-fired plants that make it the world's biggest emitter of the pollutant sulfur dioxide and the world's fifteenth-largest greenhouse emitter.

"Yes," he sighed. "So much electricity, no use."

When I asked whether he had any power at his house, Loyiso explained that his power had just been cut because he could not pay his electricity bills.

"Even before they cut it, I didn't use it. I keep all my lights off. Anything to reduce the costs," he said.

I realized then that oily smell was from the oil lamps Loyiso used to light his house and the paraffin stove he used to cook his food.

Loyiso is representative of the 43%[12] of South African households that are energy poor, meaning that they cannot meet their basic energy needs. These are usually low-income earners, who are unable to keep up with rising utility bills, or the informal settlers, who live in shacks far from Eskom's power lines.

High energy poverty in South Africa is often linked to the rise and fall of Eskom. Between 1994 and 2000, Eskom surpassed its goal of providing 1.5 million households with electricity by adding 2.4 million households to the grid. In 2007, Eskom began work on two new coal-fired stations, Medupi and Kusile, to meet growing energy demands.

However, the expected initial costs for the plants tripled, putting Eskom in financial debt. Further, corruption scandals, involving scandal-plagued ex-president Jacob Zuma and the premier consultancy firm McKinsey, not only stole vast sums of money from the company itself but also limited Eskom from raising additional capital.

Blackouts ensued. In 2007, Eskom implemented its first blackout schedule.[13] It was supposed to be a one-time stopgap. But load shedding has now become a part of South Africans' daily life.

A popular joke in South Africa goes:

"What did South Africa use before candles?"

"Electricity."

The South African government, in an attempt to revive electricity trends while tackling the environmental challenges of a coal-powered electric grid, turned to renewable sources of energy—albeit very slowly. The government developed the Renewable Energy Independent Power Producer Programme (REIPPP) in 2007. Within one decade, prices for solar photovoltaic and wind energy sources fell by 68% and 43%, respectively.[14] This is an important achievement, as cost is often a deterrent for investing in renewable energy.

Compared to other SSA countries, South Africa is unique because it had already achieved large-scale success with electricity. From its experience with a powered-up society, it understands what happens when electricity is mismanaged. South Africa can lead the renewable energy revolution on the continent with plenty of lessons learned and a passion to reestablish a once-respected energy sector.

By contrast, other SSA countries can jump straight into renewable energy, leveraging their advantage of an energy sector not tied to old ways.

From the red-hot earth crust underneath the Rift Valley in Kenya to an abundance of sunshine blazing over South Africa to the "Smoke that

Thunders" waterfall in the Zambezi River of Zambia, mother nature blesses SSA with the resources they need to meet their energy needs.

Renewable energy offers the region outsized potential to reduce pollution, decrease the dependence on fossil fuel imports, and foster economic growth and investments. The explosive potential growth in this sector represents, however, only one avenue for foreign direct investment. The leading source of capital on the continent, China, has already shifted its approach to take advantage.

Africa Needs, China Feeds

It was a full house at the UN General Assembly. Throughout the hall could be heard introductions like "President of Israel," "Your Excellency," "Governor, this way." Camera flashes captured long white robes, colorful headscarves of African women leaders, and dark suits of Western politicians.

At dinner that evening, I sat between John Mahama, the brother of the president of Ghana at the time, and the president's wife. Mahama was a talker, and he did not need much prompting before he began speaking about a business proposition. He grinned mysteriously as he shared his grand idea that I invest in his poultry business. I had to laugh. Here I was, a vegetarian, being asked by the brother to a country's president to invest in his chickens.

Mahama, like other leaders and entrepreneurs, recognizes that Africa's increasing and urbanizing population presents a huge opportunity for investors. By 2050, its population of one billion is projected to double. Eighty percent of the projected population is expected to live in the cities, bringing the urban population to more than 1.3 billion. Africa has an extremely young and able-bodied workforce, and six of the world's 12 fastest-growing economies are in SSA: Ethiopia, Democratic Republic of the Congo, Côte d'Ivoire, Mozambique, Tanzania, and Rwanda.[15]

Nonetheless, Africa cannot leap into the tech economy without first embracing new methods that increase productivity and long-term growth. For instance, with 60% of SSA's employed working in agriculture,[16] agribusiness leaders like Mahama will need to advance from low-productivity methods to a high-productivity manufacturing one—with new, advanced technologies. This cannot happen without large financial investments. Second, the continent needs to tackle corruption, both to stop the bleeding resources from growth-friendly areas, and to restore trust between people and government.

Investors often debate the double-edged effects of large foreign investments. On one hand, frontier nations stand to gain so much from abroad since local resources are limited. On the other hand, receiving large sums from other countries, what some call "handouts," may contribute to a nation's indebtedness and exacerbate corruption if money falls in the wrong hands. Sri Lanka and Pakistan are noteworthy cases in this regard.

On landing at the airports in either of these two countries, it's palpable that China "owns" these countries. It built the roadways and a disproportionate amount of the modern infrastructure. It offered loans to make this happen, which were irresistible to these economically challenged countries, and created a pattern of indebtedness and dependency. I've seen a similar China presence in other emerging market countries, sometimes most pronounced in the most remote pockets of the planet.

What's interesting to note is that the dependency has morphed into acceptance, and there is growing positive sentiment to Chinese investments. Data show that Sri Lanka trusts China and is happy with its investments, and that Pakistanis are China's strongest supporters.[17,18] For one, leadership sees Chinese systems as aligned politically with the local regime (i.e., being more authoritarian). Second, it is cheap capital, and in countries with limited alternative resources, you take what you can get.

China has plenty of investments in SSA as well. Generally, these investments are welcome, although attitudes vary among countries. I rarely hear government officials expressing fear of China, publicly accepting their money gladly. Policy leaders refer to the Chinese with respect, calling it a "friend" and "brother."

It is the taxi drivers who voice skepticism. While the politicians must be diplomatic to maintain accord in their communities, they may likewise be benefiting from direct payments. In my search for an authentic view that reflects the voice of the people and foretells the future, I often find "taxi cab confessions" to be a particularly insightful source of information.

"The people that say China is taking over Africa fail to understand that when the right hand washes the left hand, and the left hand washes the right hand, both hands become clean," a Nigerian policy leader once said to me. In his opinion, the China–Africa relationship is mutually beneficial.

In fact, China imports more from Africa than it exports.[19] Some imported products are crude oil from Angola and South Sudan, zinc and copper ore from Eritrea, cobalt from the Democratic Republic of Congo (DRC), which have all helped fuel China's rapid infrastructure development. Diamonds, cotton, and raw tobacco from Zimbabwe are some classic African products that are found in Chinese store shelves and homes.

A decade ago, Africa was my case study of a frontier region. Although it was rich with resources, cheap labor, and desire for growth, Africa did not have the income to complement these advantages. I met hundreds of prospective investors, many of whom were eager to drive the rise of Africa. They commented about the foreign presence, specifically how the Chinese were building the roadways, ports, train stations, and trade routes of Africa. I described that in building this infrastructure, they were building a backbone for African trade across the continent.

My forecast came true. At the time we spoke about the inverse: "China Needs, Africa Feeds," as China needed commodities and targeted Africa to stock up on oil and other natural resources. Today, China accesses not only traditional commodities but arguably ones even more valuable: lithium, copper, rhodium, platinum—precious metals that fuel the technology revolution.

Just as with infrastructure, China has great potential to be a transformative investor in Africa's growing digital economy. Indeed, most Africans use Chinese smartphones on a Chinese network, and at least half the time, Huawei built it.[20]

Begun in 1987, around the same time China began opening its markets, Huawei grew simultaneously with the country's growing economy. However, the company experienced the most success once it started venturing overseas. Between 2012 and 2016, Huawei made more from its international market sales than its domestic business. Even with criticism on security breaches, the company continued to record meteoric global sales, nearly one-third of which derived from international sales.[21] Huawei is championed for its ability to offer prices that are about 10% cheaper than its competitors.[22]

Most Africans are online today thanks to the cheap costs of Huawei's technology, and this relationship is bound to continue as Africa tries to meet its high connectivity demands. For example, in March

2021, Safaricom, Kenya's largest wireless carrier, launched Huawei fifth-generation wireless infrastructure.[23] With promises of Internet speeds 10 or 20 times faster than the current speed and greater connectivity, other African nations are following suit.

I worried about the risks of allying so closely with China and whether that would change my investment recommendations. History shows that trade relationships have historically left SSA disappointed. The "Dutch disease" describes how Western countries beguiled SSA, with the colonizers bidding to take control of its bountiful natural resources, including oil and precious metals.

I wondered: *When China, the right hand, washes the left hand (Africa) clean, as the Nigerian policy maker said, does the palm remain open or does it hide its intentions within a closed fist?* In other words, are the trade relationships between China and Africa mutually beneficial for both parties, or is China a harbinger of neocolonialism?

The risk of an exploitive relationship is clear, given many citations of harsh working conditions and meager pay of some Chinese companies in the region. I thought about lovely and lush Zambia as one example. The people in Zambia are warm and move slowly, reflecting the less populated, more laid-back nature of the country. The major export is mining; copper is the lifeblood of Zambia's economy. Employment is based largely within the agricultural, manufacturing, power, and construction sectors. The Chinese are omnipresent here, and concerns of gruesome labor abuses are widespread, including lack of infrastructure to prevent the crashing rock falls that can crush workers and limbs, acid burns and lung disease in workers serving 12- to 18-hour shifts in fume-filled, sulfuric tunnels without adequate respiratory gear, harsh beatings as punishments, and limited access to potable drinking water.[24]

Such down sides of China's investment in Africa are augmented by the geopolitical uncertainties of China's heavy tech investment. Africa could be caught in the crosshairs of the United States' and China's continuing technology contest—or rivalry—on global areas. For example, when the United States cut valuable supplies to Chinese telecom giant, Huawei, people feared that the global effects would be most felt in Africa's tech sector, which is a major Huawei market.

Africa has the potential to distance itself from this war by developing technologies domestically instead of being passive consumers. Nigeria is displaying growing global influence in cryptocurrency; Kenya is using drone technology to deliver medical supplies to rural villages; and all over East Africa, agritech is helping farmers to better predict weather trends and stabilize yields. The African tech ecosystem is maturing, reflecting high number of start-ups and a growing middle class.

Another concern is that African leaders could copy Beijing's Internet censorship style. Between June 2020 and May 2021, Chinese authorities have blocked several mobile apps and unauthorized virtual private networks, censored individuals who criticized China-produced vaccines, and used private messages to prosecute people who spoke out against the government, earning China the title for the seventh year of "the worst abuser of internet freedom" in 2021.[25]

I saw similar tactics when I visited Zimbabwe: every channel I tuned into displayed jovial Zimbabweans, often clad in the green, yellow, red, and black hues of the Zimbabwe flags, celebrating Mugabe. Some held placards that read, "Long live Mugabe," while others flaunted posters of Mugabe's face. The evening news was interspersed with songs written in the native Shona language, with choruses that repeatedly chanted Mugabe's name, and sometimes Mugabe's voice was played over parts of the song.

This propaganda occurred at a time when the Zimbabwe dollar was plummeting faster than the stock market crash of 1929, foreign investors were pulling their investments from the highly volatile market, and the president's 37-year rule had intensified political crisis in the nation. Put simply, 93-year-old President Mugabe was hated, but that wasn't what the media was showing. When I asked my local driver for his views, he smiled wryly and responded, "Only the good die young."

Nigeria's and China's leadership style are also often compared. Besides sharing a birthday with China (October 1), Nigeria is often criticized for running an autocratic system due to the government's overarching ability to easily change and effect new policies. In addition, like China, Nigeria's decision-making is centralized, and collectiveness is more accepted than individualism.[26]

China, though, has proven the power of a link between an autocratic style of government and technology's ability to drive progress. The Chinese have had an elaborate, deliberate strategy to invest in technology as a way to secure their global positioning into the future and as a way to account for their declining population. The autocratic government invested billions in technological innovation, and today it remains among the largest investors in tech.

In similar fashion, Nigeria is well positioned to leapfrog into the new tech economy, especially in digital currency. Even though it labors under an oppressive and corrupt government, it is executing an inexorable shift to technology. When I consider where the funding for this tech might come from, China is one of the obvious answers. Today, the adage is reversed: Africa needs (seed funding), and China feeds (with venture capital).

Can Crypto Save Nigeria?

Watching the afternoon news on October 2020 sent shivers through my body. Pitch darkness was lighted by gunshots just bright enough for me to make out people running and ducking. In the background echoed ". . .to serve . . . with love and strength and faith . . ."—parts of the Nigerian anthem, I later learned—but the bullets drowned out the chanting. Holding automatic weapons were men clad in military uniforms. I gasped as I came to the realization that the Nigerian Army was shooting at its own people.

Tagged under the video was the phrase "#ENDSARS: Protesters shot and killed in Lekki shooting." The hashtag was going viral in support of a social media–backed, decentralized movement to end police brutality in Nigeria as the newscaster shared the details of the #ENDSARS protests. The hashtag was a call for the government to end SARS (the Special Anti-Robbery Squad), a unit of the police force accused of excessive violence.

I immediately texted an old friend living in-country. "What is going on in Nigeria?" I asked, my alarm tinged with a profound sense of guilt. Incidents of this sort had to have been going on for a long time, but I was only now becoming aware of them.

"I don't know what to say," she quickly responded. "The president still hasn't said anything, and it has been 13 days already."

I understood her anger. This was not the first time the president had played a disappearing act on his people instead of addressing major issues that needed his guidance. I was reminded of a time when the government imposed capital controls and investors were on edge about losing major investments. We needed someone to explain why Nigeria was considering instituting such an extreme and unconventional policy.

Investors' tempers had flared even more when we were told that the president had left the country for a medical procedure.

During the #ENDSARS protests, the coalition FEMCO, an association of 14 young Nigerian feminist women, used their personal bank accounts to mobilize funds to support protestors. However, when the government became aware of the success of FEMCO's interventions, they ordered the country's banks to suspend bank accounts affiliated with the group.

These young leaders had brilliantly created a digital platform for raising cryptocurrency (crypto), leveraging technology to transfer authority from the government and giving it to the people—a "Robin Hood" move that was warmly received and gained them greater loyalty. It was a demonstration that "lazy Nigerian youths," as the government dubbed them, could wield their own power.[27]

Over the past generation, the government has emphasized instilling STEM (science, technology, engineering, mathematics) in education. An unintended consequence is Nigeria's youth now using technology to rebel against the government's authoritarian rule. As #EndSARS created shock waves, the youth demonstrated the power of digital capital. It also created cohorts of Nigerians who are increasingly turning to digital currency.

Nigerians also use it as an "insurance policy" to protect themselves from the country's currency mismanagement.[28] Following President Buhari's medical procedure abroad and the imposition of capital controls, local business screeched to a halt when products could no longer be imported across borders. As a result, inflation surged. Even bar soap became a luxury item; the CEO of a major consumer wares chain once told me that local store owners cut soap bars in half to compensate. Such economic crises are unfortunate for a nation with such potential. Nigeria has the largest economy in Africa and is set to be earth's largest country by population within 30 years. Many blame the government for Nigeria's turmoil, citing the rise in unemployment, inflation, and poverty during the president's first term in office. Given this tumultuous term, I was convinced that he would lose the run for presidency in 2019, but Buhari was reelected.

In the midst of this crisis, cryptocurrencies have enabled shopkeepers to skirt stifling currency controls by offering digital currency to their import partners. Trade could effectively proceed. In this example, crypto offers wealth emancipation as a rebuke to the mismanagement and corruption often tied to the naira, Nigeria's currency.

Crypto offers not only a secure digital way to access wealth, it is also fast. As an example, cryptocurrency is becoming a preferred route for foreign remittances. In 2020, remittances rose in all regions except SSA, where it fell by an astounding 12.5%. This decline was almost entirely due to a 28% decline in remittance flows to Nigerian banks.

What drove the drop in Nigeria? Ranging from emigrant husbands sending money to their families to investors sending money to procure assets back home, Nigerians in the diaspora have barely tolerated their banks because of arbitrary rates, delays, and transaction fees.[29] One could draw the link between the skyrocketing rise of crypto in Nigeria in 2020 and the atypical decrease in remittances flowing into its banks.[30]

According to a 2020 survey, 32% of respondents in Nigeria use crypto—the highest proportion of any country in the world.[31] On Bitcoin trading volume, Nigeria ranked third, trailing only behind the United States and Russia, surpassing even China.[32] In another 2021 survey, Nigeria ranked sixth in the world for overall crypto adoption.[33]

The benefits of crypto are plentiful, but it does not come without its own challenges. For a country that is synonymous with online fraud (a.k.a. the Nigerian prince scam), potential investors are wary of Nigeria's leap into digital currency. Cryptos are not regulated, thus lending an anonymity that can facilitate criminal activity. Users' assets have been hacked. Some scammers have made look-alike copies of crypto apps and fake websites, which makes assets easy to grab. Others have found a way to intercept the blockchain technology on which crypto is built, tricking it into releasing the funds stored in it without receiving legitimate permission.[34]

Nations like China have taken a draconian approach to solving the issue of crypto fraud by declaring in the last quarter of 2021 that all crypto transactions are illegal. China, and several other nations, including Nigeria, have advocated a centralized digital currency that would maintain the benefits of a digital currency without the risks of a decentralized one. In China, it is the digital yuan and in Nigeria it is the eNaira.[35]

The effect of this type of solution could be starkly different in Nigeria and China. China's yuan may be strong enough to compete against the growing crypto, but for Nigeria, the digital decentralized naira will share the same high inflation rate and abysmal devaluation rate as its paper currency.

A reasonable solution is to develop a regulatory approach that targets the blockchain technology on which crypto is built. Some of these rules could include code audits, setting risk parameters, and using artificial intelligence to monitor and circumvent suspicious activities. Other data security approaches such as using secure emails, enabling two-factor authentication, using secure Internet connections, and using strong passwords for crypto wallets could also be implemented. Ironically, this solution would depend on a strong and stable regulatory environment.

From Gray to Green: Data Is the Oil

The last decade has produced remarkable winners among frontier and emerging economies, but Nigeria stands in stark contrast. While most economies liberalized, diversified, and flourished, Nigeria's economy flatlined. Its example demonstrates clearly the burden of hanging on to old models—in this case, a dependency on its vast oil reserves, oligarchic system, and corrupted past.

As I boarded my plane for my next adventure, I glanced at the returns of various country indices. Each country was in the green but Nigeria. Not coincidentally, headlines broke about yet another terrorist attack on pipelines in the Niger Delta. Ethnic strife, poverty, and corruption fueled these attacks, and the result was increased volatility, lower investment, and distrust.

As gray smoke plumes filled the country's southern sky, I glanced eastward out my window to see dozens of geometric circles of green farmland irrigated and plowed in synchronous motion. My seatmate, a young man with a charming accent and Adidas sweatshirt, noticed my gaze. He pulled out his phone to show his Ag Tech designs that would transform the country. His technology would crowdsource funds for farmers, enabling the broader population to participate in the country's natural prosperity, providing predictable funding streams for farmers, and helping to ensure food security for the burgeoning population.

Caught between the distress of the Nigerian assets plummeting and the excitement for his vision, I could see before my eyes what it means for data to be the new oil. While oil's discovery had brought corruption, data brings transparency. While oil concentrates wealth, data is distributive in nature. While oil literally combusts the earth's crust, data is the ultimate renewable and regenerative resource.

As the Global South is projected to be home to the majority of megacities within years, SSA countries are taking advantage of their freedom to adapt. Like so many emerging markets, their transition into a new world of prosperity is taking place over years as opposed to decades. What was once regarded as the Dark Continent may soon become a beacon lighting the way to the future – maybe, for us all.

8

Twenty-First Century Investing

Transforming Economies and Livelihoods from Bogotá to Brasilia

On landing in Bogotá to attend my friend's wedding, I encountered a militarized airport with soldiers in fatigues and tanks lining the passenger loading zones. I worked my way to a taxi, and once we hit the road, my driver careened down the streets into the dark night. I could see over the seat that he had one hand on the wheel and the other on a gun.

As we sped through the dark streets, I noted that he raced through a red light and then another. After holding my breath through the first two, I asked him, "*Por qué? Qué pasa?*" trying to limit the anxiety in my voice.

His looked at me in his rearview mirror, and he quietly but sternly replied, in a thick accent, "No. We don't stop when it's red."

I understood at once. I'd heard the stories of travelers being stopped, robbed, kidnapped, and worse. With a big gulp, I realized that this time it could be me.

Kidnappings were endemic in the country at the time. People were held for months or years while their families tried to raise the money to pay for their release. A stop at a red light gave kidnappers enough time to descend, pull you from a car, and spirit you away.

The wedding events were held at my hotel, and I was pleased to spend the bulk of the trip within its beautiful and heavily guarded confines. We had a blast.

Two days later, my friend and I ventured out to visit the luxurious Termales los Volcanes hot springs in nearby Macheta. Shortly after enjoying the warm, soothing waters, I fell sick. I began vomiting uncontrollably. When we arrived at the airport, I was still sick. My friend found a wheelchair, and she carted me through the airport in it.

As we went through the security lines, I was detained. My Spanish was not great, and my eyes were rolling back in my head, but I tried to smile. I weakly implored, "*Por favor.*" I added unconvincingly, "*Yo estoy bien.*" It was a very confused and broken conversation as I told them I needed to be on that plane.

The agent called others over. They spoke with my friend to understand where we had visited, why we were here, where we were going. They opened my bags and looked through my papers to find my Wharton school binders and reading material.

Finally, the agents let us go. I could feel their eyes on me until we boarded the plane. Miraculously, once I got on that flight, my symptoms cleared.

Then I realized what had happened. The agents thought I was sick because I was a "drug mule" smuggling cocaine. It was common for pellets of cocaine to be wrapped in condoms and swallowed by people, especially women. If any of those wrappers came loose en route, the huge shot of cocaine would be enough to make anyone sick, or even to overdose and die.

My illness was a grim reminder of the battle between drug cartels and the government for control of Colombia. That was hardly a promising environment for foreign investment.

Historically referred to as "banana republics," Latin American countries have a sordid history of military-backed coups, corruption, and civil unrest. So it is ironic that the region has emerged in recent years as a haven of peace and safety across the globe. As a traveling investor, I sought to understand what factors ultimately drive such a transformation. If I could predict these measures, perhaps I could pick the next big market opportunity.

Doing Good and Doing Well in Colombia

Colombia is a perfect example of how economic and social transformation can drive massive gains for early investors. For many, the image of the country is still tied to its history of crime, drugs, and civil war. The drug kingpin Pablo Escobar defined old Colombia. One of seven kids of an elementary school teacher, he got his start in crime selling counterfeit high school diplomas in the 1960s. By the time he was killed by police in 1993, he had built an empire on cocaine, amassing $30 billion, the equivalent of $64 billion in 2021. He was the wealthiest criminal in history.[1]

What many people don't know is that he was also a politician. Escobar was elected to the Chamber of Representatives of Colombia in 1982 and advocated building houses and creating community centers across the country. He became beloved by many Colombians, who were willing to overlook his cartel's murdering of police officers, judges, and rivals. He had made Colombia the murder capital of the world.[2] When Escobar was killed after a nationwide manhunt in 1993,[3] his death did not deflate his paradoxical legendary status. More than 25,000 Colombians attended his funeral, and his house was transformed into a theme park.

Less than a decade later, I joined the investment banking group at Goldman Sachs, and we were looking for deals. The head of my project was a Colombian banker, and he could see that the private sector in Latin America was primed for change. With his long, wavy hair, and trendy, fun-loving fashion, Carlos didn't look the part of a buttoned-up investment banker. Carlos towered over his teammates, with his tall lanky frame and tall, black, lace-up leather boots. Carlos told me, "When it comes to Colombia, things are no longer what they seem."

For years I chased after Carlos and his far-flung ideas as he spurred deals throughout the region. I was his analyst, covering energy assets and modeling financials, while he uncovered pockets of opportunity. Carlos could see budding entrepreneurs and established businesspeople alike looking for capital, looking for growth.

As Carlos ventured on trip after trip, he would tell me, "Asha, there's opportunity here! You just have to come!"

I had experienced the effects of Colombia's violence firsthand, but Carlos showed me a new version that was thirsty for capital and had deep, vacant wells to fill. With cash-rich banking reserves in the United States, our clients, several large integrated oil and gas companies, were intrigued. Carlos structured deals that would have been inconceivable just a few years prior. To me, Carlos was an innovator and an artist, a banker, and a visionary.

A few short years later, I was running the frontier portfolio at Acadian Asset Management. Looking for an edge, I pored over recent history to identify trends and novel themes. For weeks I stared at my computer screen, pulling up datasets, asking questions, and answering them with charts and graphs. No matter how I cut the data, Colombia stood out boldly.

In 2010, one of the major benchmark providers upgraded its classification from frontier to emerging market status. It was the first-ever "upgrade" among any entity. Soon active and passive investors alike poured capital into this country's previously undiscovered investment potential. Colombia's returns soared, outpacing its developed and emerging market peers. An investment in Colombia's growth was a no-brainer.

While many experienced analysts spoke of Colombia as a failed state, the returns begged a different story. Yes, the nation's history of extreme violence, including bombings and assassinations, had exploded in the 1980s. Yes, narcotics traffickers controlled about a third of Colombian territory. And, yes, wealthy, educated Colombians had fled the country in droves. But those facts were all indicative of the past. By any forward-looking measure, Colombia was undergoing transition.

By the end of the aughts, Colombia had ended its drug war, signed a historic peace deal, and rose to be the singular success story of Latin America in every way: a strong economy, dramatic returns, climate preparedness, exciting and new-age investment platforms, and, remarkably, a bastion of peace and prosperity. Colombia had finally healed from its own illness, turning the corner into a new era of social and economic progress.

I confidently doubled my own investments in the country, and Colombia became the first dramatic success story of my career.

■ ■ ■

Most Latin American countries have struggled economically over the past decade. Brazil is perpetually the country of tomorrow. Argentina has lurched from one abysmal year to the next; like Venezuela, it only seems to move backward. Colombia is the bright exception, and it offers an interesting case study on Latin American markets and their potential for growth.

Given its small geographical size, people sometimes assume that it is not one of the major South American countries. But with 50 million inhabitants, it is the second most populous country on the continent.

This disconnect is reflected in the equity market, where Colombia makes up less than 1% of the Morgan Stanley Capital International's emerging markets index.[4]

Colombia is an excellent example of how a resource-dependent country with a history of bad governance, incessant war, rampant crime, and a volatile stock market can find a pathway ahead. Its economy is sound. And while violence occasionally breaks out, the rate of homicides is less than one-third relative to 1991.[5]

How did Colombia turn around so swiftly?

The process started with its people deciding that they had had enough. In 2008, over a million Colombians joined together for a nationwide protest, collectively stating "*No más*" to the Revolutionary Armed Forces of Colombia (FARC).

Colombia elected a new president, whose business-friendly policies would spur private investment, infusing capital into its rapidly changing economy. Alvaro Uribe, who stayed in office until 2010, when term limits prevented him from running again, emphasized the critical importance of maintaining peace. In speeches to his constituents, Uribe would say, "We cannot prosper, we cannot advance in investment, if we continue being a country with a high level of insecurity." He understood that private investments are imperative to growth, but the level of investment needed to grow Colombia would be impossible without first making it safer for all citizens.[6]

Uribe was tough on crime. During his administration, Colombia tripled its defense budget to nearly $12 billion, and the national police presence spread through all 1,300 municipalities. Strengthened security and improved intelligence reduced kidnappings from 3,000 in 2000 to just over 200 in 2009.[7] In an effort to disrupt cartel leadership, 1,300 Colombians accused of drug charges were extradited to the United States.[8]

During the same time the president went after foreign capital in the form of trade deals. When Uribe took office in 2002 Colombia's foreign direct investment was just over $2 billion; by 2008, that number soared to more than $10 billion.[9] Uribe oversaw both economic and social reforms. During the initial years, as violence was reduced, the percentage of funding for sustainable economic development increased. As examples, government funding covered the planting of 350,000 hectares of farmland to provide benefits for thousands of farmers, establishing more than

100 justice centers supporting over a thousand community-led projects valued at $487 million, and providing reparations to 600,000 victims of violence.[10] Further, despite its energy-rich reserve base, Colombia led the world stage by becoming only one of two emerging economies (alongside China) to implement a tax on carbon emissions.

Colombia's financial investments in peace, people, and planet had massive economic payoffs. Its quick recovery from the global recession of 2007–2008 was driven by consumption, internal demand, low interest rates, and investment in the oil and mining sectors, which soared as rebel violence decreased. As security increased, foreign direct investments flowed into Colombia, especially in medium-sized cities where the bulk of the population lives.

Why did these assets flow? Investors, including myself, were witnessing before our eyes a market that was truly emerging. The peasants who were offered land were soon able to afford Happy Meals—with actual toys. (In my early coverage, I spoke with the management team of Arcos Dorados, "Golden Arches," who explained that importing Chinese toys was too expensive, so instead they included locally made paper books.) The middle class was able to afford larger purchases, and the number of cars on the street increased by 600% over that period.[11]

As for its government, Colombia remains the longest running democracy in the region. Its stability increased to the point that, in 2017, the FARC agreed to a peace deal and handed in their weapons to the United Nations. Now they're a political party, committed to eradicating poverty through communist means and land reform.[12] They call themselves "The Commons."

Colombia's economic stability has been reinforced by an integrated social protection system, covering health, social security, and education, along with policies that seek to emphasize education and reduce inequality. Its reduction in its poverty rate—9.3 million of its citizens were lifted out of poverty between 2010 and 2018—has been one of the fastest in the world. The country today is prosperous, urban, and modern—a magnet for investment. It's transitioned from a commodity-based to a demand-led economy.

The results have improved not only the quality of life for its citizens, but also the business environment for local leaders and international investors. Its success does raise a question, however. Why haven't other countries in the region, especially the large ones with a better head start, performed as well?

The Role of Business in Argentina's Society

There is little disagreement that Argentina has been the Great Short of the last decade. Once the tenth wealthiest nation in the world based on GDP per capita, it has tumbled to seventy-third place.[13, 14]

A primary reason is the country's populist philosophy, personified by recurring and polarizing leader, former two-term president, Cristina Fernández de Kirchner. The wife of another former Argentine president, she set price controls, saddled the country with crippling debt by offering handouts, nationalized valuable bona fide businesses, lowered the minimum voting age to 16 in a ploy to win reelection, advocated for a three-term amendment, and was even accused of a grisly murder of a political dissident. Under President Kirchner's leadership, Argentina received the largest bailout ever from the International Monetary Fund, $57 billion—not a laudable statistic. Her policies of emptying government coffers sent inflation soaring to nearly 25%. Over the last decade, the country's progress came to a screeching halt under her leadership and then toppled.

Her political challenges became personal to me in the fall of 2018. One of the companies I followed was acquired by a competitor, resulting in a handsome premium for investors. It was important to realize the premium and pass the gains along. However, the transaction was held up in the courts. Argentine regulators wouldn't let investors sell the stock until the ruling was complete. In my broken, Portuguese-laden Spanish, I called the courthouse to learn more. *When would the judge decide? Why was the transaction held up? Was there anything I could do?* I soon learned the judge was distracted. He was working on a case related to Kirchner's association to a murdered associate. The Kirchner-Nisman case? He would be distracted for years.

I decided to connect with a consortium of the few investors who were willing to invest in Argentine companies at this time. We banded together to write a letter in which we explained our situation and pleaded for action. We politely warned that we would call the media, both locally and in the United States, if action were not taken soon. Argentina was seeking an upgrade to emerging market at the time. Its case for an up-grade was tenuous, and negative publicity would not help. The authorities caved. Within days the judge's gavel hit the desk; the transaction was ap-proved, and the investors' returns were realized.

What lessons did I take away from this mess? (1) I learned the pow-er of collaborative investment stewardship. By aggregating the power of our voices and our billions of dollars in assets, we made people listen—especially company leaders and governments. (2) Argentinian courts are mired in politics, and Christina Kirchner was a quack. In the twenty-first century, sophisticated wars are fought behind computers, not in populist gimmicks and twentieth-century guerilla warfare.

A third lesson was gained not from this story but another one, a fabulous success story. While Argentina was the weakest stock market performer of all countries, it is the home of a consumer tech company, MercadoLibre. This company's stock was one of the top 10 returning securities across the full 40,000 stocks traded in every country around the globe.[15] MercadoLibre's market value has become bigger than any country within its index.

I had been following its development from the very beginning—on campus at Stanford in the late 1990s. As an undergraduate, I saw the In-ternet boom take off. Regularly, friends of mine would "stop out" or even drop out of school to work for Google, Yahoo!, PayPal, and other red-hot Internet companies—most of which no longer exist today.

In dorms rooms and over lunch, kids would get together to ideal-ize how the current physical world could be made virtual. There was a palpable sense that everything around us would move to the Internet age—the libraries, the way we socialized, education, and even commerce and money itself. The hard part, as always, was the execution.

Across campus, in the MBA building, one student decided to go for it. He could see not only the opportunity of the Internet itself but also how it could fully transform economic development in the developing world. Marcos Galperin was an Argentine student who saw the pieces come together: low cost of labor, large untapped talented labor pool, high unmet needs in a country with limited infrastructure, and rapidly growing spending power.

His vision of the Latin American "free market" transformed into the literally translated MercadoLibre.[16] Within Galperin's first three months building his company, MercadoLibre gained 15,000 users. Within a year it expanded to Brazil, Uruguay, and Mexico.[17] I like to call it the "Amazon of the Amazon." Others call the company the "eBay of Latin America." In fact, eBay bought into the company and formed a partnership.

I met Galperin and his chief financial officer (CFO), not in a Bay Area coffee shop, but thousands of miles south, in a small conference room in the city of Good Air, Argentina's capital—Buenos Aires. At that point MercadoLibre was not yet the largest and most popular e-commerce site in Latin America. The office building was large and sat mostly vacant in an unpopulated office park. The two young men were bouncing with energy. I felt that I was back at the Stanford CoHo (Coffee House) sitting among friends, as they laid out their vision. "Argentine talent is underappreciated," they said. They walked me through their sources of untapped talent pools, and before long I had no doubt this large office space would be bustling in no time.

As we sipped strong, black Argentine coffee, they described the potential impact of their ideas. To them, the company represented more than this year's sales and next quarter's earnings. It had the potential to expand to the most remote villages and bring in marginalized people to participate in the global economy. Their ultimate goal was to democratize commerce and build their clients' wealth through entrepreneurship.

Marcos spoke of the changes as a "revolution." He believed that they could help people bring themselves out of poverty if only they had a platform. I left his office impressed and inspired. A Silicon Valley start-up was flourishing right here, couched between the Andes mountain range and the Atlantic Ocean.

Marcos Galperin's vision has proved itself. Since the time of that meeting, the stock price of MercadoLibre has soared 1,200% in a 10-year span. In 2020, at the height of the tech boom, the company grew so large that its weight in the S&P Frontier index was literally higher than that of any country within it.

Today, more than 200,000 families rely on sales through MercadoLibre for most or all of their household income. As Galperin's company grosses billions and billions of dollars each year, he continues to speak of his vision about democratizing access, creating jobs, and equalize opportunity. Marcos has created a case study of how technology and vision can create firms that generate both returns and impact.

To return to the third lesson I learned, it is precisely this. Marcos's situation vis-à-vis Argentina is not alone. In this era of "stakeholder capitalism," companies are increasingly called upon to define their "corporate purpose" and to maintain social progress and well-being.

Why? Companies represent the bulk of employment around the world. Accountable to shareholders, companies are nimble in decision-making and efficient in resource allocation. Companies more typically than governments have access to modern technology and consumer research, as these tools are needed to enable bottom-line results. Ultimately, businesses have the infrastructure and processes to make change happen quickly when needed.

Some corporations have grown so enormous that they've eclipsed the GDP of large countries. At the time of this writing, Apple, for example, has a market cap of $2.1 trillion, larger than the GDPs of Canada, Italy, and Russia. Microsoft's, with $1.9 trillion, is larger than those of Brazil, Korea, and Australia. If these companies were countries, they would rank in the top 10 largest economies in the world.[18]

As corporations grow larger than countries both in size and scale, what role will they play? This question is relevant throughout the globe. Two-thirds of the S&P 500 companies are multinational companies, spanning the globe for raw materials, labor, and customers. To whom are they accountable?

The "free market" capitalist model does more than boost returns. It has a reinforcing mechanism that drives impact as well. We have seen that more than 200,000 families rely on sales through MercadoLibre for most or all of their household income. Companies are increasingly called upon to maintain social order and well-being. Why? Companies represent the bulk of employment around the world. Accountable to shareholders, companies are nimble in decision-making and efficient in resource allocation. Their competitive pressures require investments in modern technology and consumer research. Ultimately, businesses have the infrastructure and processes to make change happen quickly when needed.

This development is not new. There are countless examples from history of the private sector utilizing the power of their capital to drive broad social impact. The godfather of modern capitalism himself, Milton Friedman, who declared that the business of business is business, said, "It may well be in the long-run interest of a corporation that is a major employer in a small community to devote resources to providing amenities to that community or to improving its government. That may make it easier to attract desirable employees."

> Friedman's philosophy was later reflected in a pragmatic framework. Harvard Business School guru, Michael E. Porter, whose "Five Forces" framework has been taught to most business school graduates over the past four decades, explicitly states that companies' market strength is determined by its commitment to broader social needs, citing specifically company positioning relative to suppliers, customers, and employees.
>
> One key stakeholder, government, understands the capacity of the private sector. For instance, when African governments were struggling to deliver refrigeration-dependent vaccines to remote areas, Coca-Cola leveraged its distribution network. The initiative, called Project Last Mile,[19] combines supply chain logistics with humanitarian efforts to distribute medication to areas the governments can't reach on their own.[20]
>
> In the case of Argentina, we see a government that has tanked its economy while its largest company is in effect doing the work of the government in helping people. What is an investor to do? In terms of social good, the company is providing a greater return on investment.

From Destruction to Disruption in Brazil

Two thousand miles north of Argentina's breathtaking Cerro de los Siete Colores (or "Hill of the Seven Colors") lies the Amazon River and the world's largest virgin rainforest. In my early 20s, I fell in love with the country. I spent my final semester at Stanford in northeast Brazil, near the great historical city of Salvador, in a small, isolated beach town called Maceio. I still refer to the region as *paraismo*, paradise. I visited the region again and again for many years, traversing from the coast into the heart of the Amazon rain forest to a then-under-trafficked city called Manaus.

When I was a recent graduate, having completed my degrees in cultural anthropology and natural sciences, the Amazon rain forest was a mesmerizing haven—from the lush biodiversity with potential for biomedical applications to the serenity of the forest to the vibrancy in its canopy. For a student of evolutionary biology, it was fascinating to observe the continual fight for life and the natural strategic instincts of all life forms—from insects to bushes to aboriginal people and immigrants.

I secured work at an electronics plant in an opportunity zone just outside Manaus. I built business plans and strategized the future of the region, observing investors and philanthropists alike who were exploring the region. I spent my weekends in Vivenda, a peaceful riverside town far from the bustle of the Amazon capital.

On the Friday evening drive to the cottage, the warm air would embrace my friends and me as we steered down the straight, narrow, wet, never-ending, freshly paved forest roads. Sunlight sifted gently through the trees soaring overhead. The lush vegetation and deep pink clay showed through where the black asphalt roads ended, exuding mineral richness. The evolutionary solutions in this vast, untouched land were breathtaking.

What impassioned me most was to think about the analogies for humans in this environment. I'd wonder, *how can humans, with our different beginnings, strengths, and goals, co-exist harmoniously?*

Like America, Brazil is a melting pot—the locals are a mix of native people. Some have lived isolated for thousands of years in the forest, alongside generations of European immigrants, African slaves, and their intermixed descendants. But unlike America, the color of one's skin didn't seem to matter. Alongside the Amazon River, I'd watch boys and girls play soccer in the sand and splash in the water. Their lean bodies would glisten in the sunlight, and I'd marvel at their internal rhythms. My hips could never do what theirs could. From afar, all their colors seemed the same. In this part of the country, to me, colors merged. Dark brown, medium brown, light brown—everyone was some shade of another's, and they would salsa and samba in a brilliant sea of gorgeous tan, luminous skin. It felt as though, *here skin color has no significance.*

While the setting before me was idyllic, it was juxtaposed against a violent history, an extractive present, and a corrupt future. During these drives, we would listen to Elis Regina, a jazz diva with a fiery, throaty voice, and Antonio Jobim, considered the father of Bossa Nova, as they pleaded for peace and freedom from military rule. For me they represented the youthful, unstoppable energy of Brazil, protesting against its painful, brutal past. They would sing of the "identification cards" that people had to carry to leave their homes a short generation earlier.

Failure to show them on demand would risk their families, their homes, and their lives.

Out my window, the thick, fruity smell of the rain forest would be overlaid with the scent of smoke wafting through the forest. A nearby logging operation was clearing the land with wildfires, and the faint hum of chainsaws provided an unlikely background amid the chirps and buzz of the natural forest.

Far to the south, I knew my Goldman Sachs partners were on site advising the leadership of Petrobras. During this period, the country's oil company leadership and government officials engaged in a corruption scandal that laundered money through Rolexes, private beachfront apartments, and even a hackneyed car wash. The scandal cost shareholders more than $5 billion, thousands of Brazilians lost their jobs, construction companies went bankrupt, and the president of the country was jailed.

That was not an isolated incident. Brazil has been rife with environmental problems. In 2016, a dam burst in southeastern Mariana City, and not only rainwater flooded out. The dam was holding toxic wastewater from an iron ore mine. Toxic mud overwhelmed a couple of nearby villages.

Approximately 600 people were evacuated, and 19 were killed. One of the dead was a five-year-old child, the same age as my Jasper at the time. He was found after being washed ashore 40 miles downstream.[21] When I learned about it, I felt a sharp ache as I thought of the child's mother.

The company that owned the dam, Vale, is an international behemoth, Brazil's second largest company and one of the 10 largest metals and mining companies on earth. In a show of support, the company coined a motto: "Mariana, Never Again!"

The motto didn't have much staying power.[22] Less than four years later, hundreds of mine workers were in a cafeteria eating lunch in the city of Brumandinho when millions of tons of toxic, biohazard mud burst through the building. Approximately 270 people died, a railway bridge was destroyed, and the nearby Paraopeba River was contaminated all the way to the Atlantic Ocean.

The cause? A local dam experienced a spectacular failure. As a result, Vale was forced to pay $7 billion in compensation, and 16 people associated with Vale were charged with homicide and environmental offenses.[23,24] Vale claimed that they were doing everything in their power to prevent another burst dam, while federal police accused them of falsifying documents in Brumadinho about the dam's stability. Perhaps more devastatingly to the company, the company's reputation was tarnished, and its value dropped $19 billion.[25]

Here was the dark face, as MercadoLibre has been a bright side, of an international behemoth. As an investor, how could I ensure this type of disaster wouldn't happen again? One might assume I wouldn't have any effect over Brazilian business governance, but it wasn't true. As one of the larger foreign investors in Brazil, I represented one of the people that Brazilian companies would listen to. And for me, this one felt personal.

As a "voice of ESG," a large investor in the country, and a personal devotee to this region, I was called to action. I joined 100 of my investing peers under a collaborative initiative, organized by the Church of England, to pool our assets. In total, it amounted to an immense $14 trillion dollars. Together, we demanded transparency. We wanted to ensure that we'd be aware of other risks and that we'd be positioned to take action before another disaster. With that much capital, who was better positioned to hold companies like Vale accountable?

As a coordinated group, we emailed company CEOs, CFOs, and investor-relations executives. We wanted details on the mining operations of nearly 1,000 mining companies all over the world. It was a bold message and, because of the dollar amount, not one that these companies could easily shrug off.

To be fair, compliance has been less than complete. As of this writing, only about a third of those companies have responded. However, 45 of the 50 largest mining companies have given us information about more than 1,800 tailings dams.[26] The information has been gathered on a public, searchable database where anyone, whether citizen, investor, or environmentalist, can access it. Perhaps just as important, the pressure has encouraged a global review of safety standards for tailings dams. New protocols launched in 2020 demand that dams cause no harm to people, no harm to the environment, and result in no loss of human life.[27]

In the twentieth century, this type of action was unheard of. Shareholder activism is emerging as a powerful tool to align the priorities of planet, people, prosperity, and profits.

A sustainability revolution is surging, and investors are one critical source of this sweeping change. But there's another critical driver as well.

Chile: Accelerating into the Future

We live in the era of big data. Today, not only is it easier to communicate with one another, it's also easier to track each other, to draw statistical relationships, and to be more proactive. With the sustainability movement now mainstream, and the dramatic emergence of many markets, we can see transformation occurring before our eyes.

But we can see exceptions too. Every anecdote seems to have a counterpoint. As an investor, how do I know when "people's interest" and profits align? Phrased differently, when is investing for sustainability simply "good karma," and when is it financially material?

Revolutions are occurring throughout the continent. For years I have followed Chile as an investment opportunity. The beautiful mountainous country is well known for two distinctive features: (1) fine wine, enabled by its fortunate topography, long coast line, and history of Spanish and French winemakers in the region, as well as (2) remarkably strong governance standards. The country boasts the highest GDP per capita in the region of US$25,891 (purchasing power parity), which stands high above its peers in the UN's Human Development Index. It also leads the emerging markets in transparency and corruption, and it leads the continent in the Digital Evolution Index.

Despite this enviable positioning, the country experienced its own unrest in 2019. In early October, the public transport authorities raised fares for buses and metros. A group of high schoolers coordinated a backlash in a social media campaign that they dubbed, "Evade!"

Within weeks, the protest swelled. The protestors expanded from a small pool of Santiago's disenchanted secondary school students to more than a million people throughout the country. The issue scaled as well because bus fares were only one example of Chile's vast inequality. While the country was the continent's wealthiest, that wealth poured into the hands of only a few. Overall, wide gaps existed—disadvantaging women, the indigenous, and the systemically poor.

The youth demanded more, and they got it.

The protest lasted months and only subsided when the revolution was completed. The president was forced to accept a new social order, and the country's constitution was fully rewritten.

It is a big deal for a well-governed, well-established democracy to rewrite its constitution. The new version addresses healthcare, inequality, water rights, and environmental protection, all top among the list of protestors' concerns.[28] When the people of Chile voted on who would draft the new constitution, an astounding 79% voted to include gender parity measures for the delegates, ensuring that half of the 155 delegates would be women.

By social measures, a once strong country appears only stronger. A friend and fellow Wharton graduate, Robert Moreno Heimlich, who represents one of Chile's largest banks, shared with me the tremendous strides they've made. His firm has achieved gender diversity at both its management committee and board levels. The bank invests heavily in social inclusion, offering low-cost loans, accessible technology, and even office space to the poor.

With the backing of today's sustainability movement by investors, Rodrigo asked me, pleadingly, "Why hasn't Chile been rewarded?" Despite all the progress, Chile's returns had only faltered. "Why are we penalized?"

There is a range of reasons. For one, sustainability takes place only over a long cycle. The payoffs occur only after the foundation is built and the economic gains can be realized. Separately, not all sustainable shifts are financially "material." Seminal research has shown that only a subset of traditional ESG measures result in measurable financial benefit.

But technology and sustainability have the opportunity to do more than drive financial results. They can rebuild the system itself.

With more data available and a broader understanding of how interlinked our systems are, we should recategorize what productivity and wellness actually mean. For example, one of the most established measures to estimate a country's potential is gross domestic product (GDP) or its cousin, gross national product (GNP). These measures include broad economic measures such as national incomes, savings, credit purchases, commodity production, and accumulation of capital.

GDP became a widely used measure following the Great Depression, helping governments evaluate the recovery across economies. However, the measure's pioneer and Nobel Prize winner, Simon Kuznets, cautioned the US Congress himself about its usefulness. In 1937 he insisted, "The welfare of a nation can scarcely be inferred from . . . GDP."

Those words have even more resonance 70 years later. GDP has proven to be an inadequate and flawed measure. First, it is ineffective to investors in predicting a market return because it's at best a concurrent indicator and more likely a lagging one. A better measure would consider social effects and unemployment, equality, wellness, environmental stability, ease of doing business, the interplay businesses have with the government, and trust in institutions.

Second, the perceived value of "growth at any cost" is waning, evidenced most starkly by China's recent policy change to a "stable growth" agenda. That enables growth, at a slower rate, and prioritizes market stability, a clean environment, and a strong middle class. As countries change their economic objectives toward stability and regeneration, our economic measures will likely change too.

A number of attempts have been made: (1) The Human Development Index, developed by the United Nations, which considers education, health and longevity, and per capita income; (2) Green Gross Domestic Product and Gross Sustainable Development Product, which assess the impact economic growth has on the environment; (3) the Better Life Index, developed by the Organisation for Economic Co-operation and Development (OECD), considers economic measures (housing spending, income, and jobs) alongside quality of life (social support network, education, and environmental quality)[29]; (4) the Gross Happiness Index, developed by Bhutan's fourth Dragon King Jigme Singye Wangchuck and adopted by the United Nations in 2011, measures a range from physical well-being and standard of living to education and ecological diversity.[30]

While none of these has gained mass traction, the latest iteration, the Sustainable Development Goals, developed by the United Nations, is rapidly being tracked by the private sector.

Data change everything. To be fair to Kuznets, if we had access to data then like we have now, we might have developed a different measure. In fact, if we had today's technologies that can measure intangibles and social welfare in the 1930s, we might never have adopted the static GDP measure at all.

With these measures in place, we can wonder, *What will the future look like?* Policy makers and corporate incentives may shift, marginalized populations may be activated, technologies may be unlocked, and economies may ignite. With a recalibrated set of measures, will Latin America's markets take off? Can Brazil truly be the country of tomorrow?

Greenlighting Latin America

Latin America's markets show the different lessons that have been learned from their pasts. Populist uprisings bring unrest to nations, and growth that doesn't support the masses inherently puts leadership at risk. The crumbling of Venezuela, the persistent downgrades of Argentina, and the serial impeachment of Brazil's presidents offer cases on the negative side.

Yet when social objectives align with the private sector's objectives, what can happen? In Colombia, it's almost uncanny how the merger of the two has led to its emergence. Despite the setbacks and obstacles, the Colombian people have persevered, continuing to move toward growth and progress. In Chile, a nationwide protest produced further equality for its citizens.

Examples can be found within countries as well. In Brazil, pockets of opportunity are emerging, especially as FinTech is changing the landscape. To enable financial empowerment and access, the country's central bank liberalized its standards, easing capital requirements and allowing FinTechs to run their own payment collection and lending services. As a result, Brazil is now the fifth-largest FinTech market in the world, and nearly 10% of its population—14 million Brazilians—was brought into the banked economy in 2020.[31,32]

Having long shed their "banana republic" past of military rule and desolate poverty, Latin America, and emerging markets broadly, are the fastest growing, most dynamic markets across the globe. Colombia, Chile, and other emerging markets in Latin America give investors the opportunity to regard investments differently than we have in the past. Investors can play an important role in directing the growth that will impact millions of people for decades to come. Latin America is no stranger to hardship, but it is also rich in opportunity for prosperity among the masses.

Brazil's famous Encontro das Águas, or "Meeting of the Waters," a place of swirling color where the black waters of the Rio Negre converge with the silty, yellow Solimões River, symbolizes this rich, magical continent. The two waters, different in their makeup, temperature, and rate of flow, run alongside each other, together yet separate, for nearly three miles until they finally blend into the lower Amazon basin, indistinguishable from each other.

In the same way, local peoples and governments can work together with corporations and investors. Each has its role, and while each move at a different pace, we can bring different skills and assets to bear. Eventually, our co-working creates a symbiotic network that benefits not just one country or one investor but the broader ecosystems in which we co-exist.

Beijing, China. The surveillance economy meets the emulation economy. These guards summed up China for me. When I photographed them in traditional attire, they unabashedly turned their cameras back on me.

Shopping at the two yuan (approximately one quarter) store in Beijing. China rapidly grew from an imitation economy to a geopolitically threatening hotbed of innovation.

Binh Duong, Vietnam. The Dairy Queen, Chairman General Director Mai Kieu Lien, embodies Vietnam's rapidly growing economy: a dynamic fusion of her manufacturing prowess, large and youthful consumer set, and social and ecological balance.

Source: Vinamilk Việt Nam: Nâng tầm sữa Việt bằng công nghệ tự động hóa – IA Vietnam

Hanoi, Vietnam. Banging the gong at the Hanoi Stock Exchange. For the last decade, Vietnam has been the darling of frontier investors.

Riyadh, Saudi Arabia. Unexpected sights: two women without the hijab, one investor (myself) and one princess (Her Royal Highness Princess Haifa Mohammed Alsaud, both in support of bringing tourism and a liberated perspective to this burgeoning region.

Bucharest, Romania. When hard communism falls to hard capitalism, a residential building in Romana Square is decorated with commercial advertisements

Kuwait City, Kuwait. Standing alongside my father and Kuwaitis at the country's House of National Works. With the fall of Saddam Hussein following the US invasion of Iraq, jubilant Kuwaits were eager to capture his head. Shown here is the head of the statue that stood in Firdos Square, Baghdad.

Lucknow, India. My first internship was in microfinance, offering small loans to entirely female borrowing groups. The power of this (limited) capital was to enable them to build business, support their families, secure independence, and nurture their communities.

Herat, Afghanistan. A boy smiles with solar panels to heat water in his backdrop. The future is global, tech-enabled, and sustainable.
Source: UNICEF / UNI309803 / Frank Dejongh

Harare, Zimbabwe. Following hyperinflation in 2009, 200,000 in local Zimbabwe Dollars was not worth a loaf of bread. As inflation and the black market continue to haunt the continent's monetary value, some investors look to cryptocurrencies as the solution.
Source: ASSOCIATED PRESS

Accra, Ghana. Selorm Adadevoh, educated and trained in the US and now CEO of MTN Ghana, breaks ground alongside Ghana's Vice President Mahamudu Bawumi on the Tamale SHS Girls dormitory, highlighting the role of corporations in delivering social impact. | Photos (ghanaweb.com)

Lima, Peru. Envisioning a sustainable economy, balancing prosperity, peace, dignity for all, and our ecological landscape. How will we use to-day's tech-enabled solutions to better measure a healthy economy?

Source: Elijah Nouvelage / Alamy Stock Photo

Boston, MA. The author poses alongside former US Treasurer, Rosie Rios. Rios remarked on the irony that the largest emerging market in the world is also the largest population in the world.

New York, NY. Following election night with UN Secretary General, Antonio Guterres remarked on how technology brings voice to the people and opportunity to bring our planet into balance. Global investors and policy makers share a responsibility to invest in the ecosystem in which we wish to live.

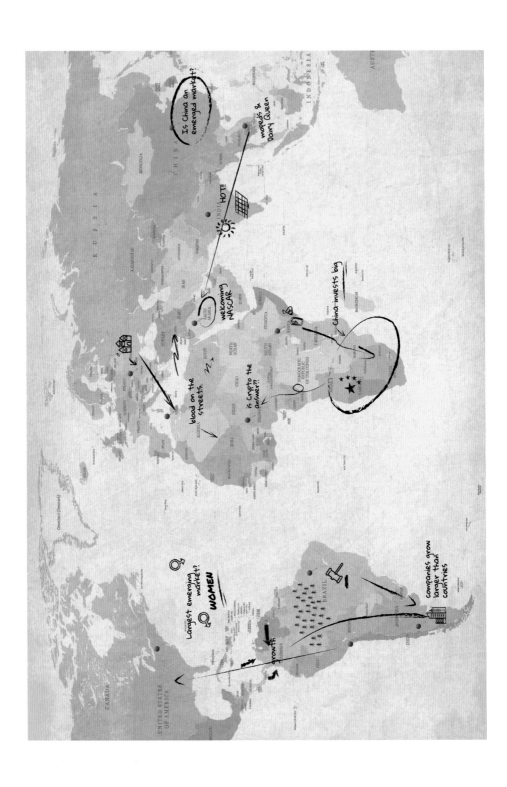

9

The Next Half: The Queens of Wall Street

The Largest Emerging Market Is Women

On a warm summer evening in Boston, I sat across from UN Ambassador Madeleine Albright. I shared my experiences as an early investor in Saudi Arabia, where deliberate building of the stock market has resulted in economic change at lightning speed. She too had observed economic progress, and she suggested it extended to social norms as well. She quipped, "Dealing with men in Saudi Arabia is nothing compared to dealing with the men in Washington." In guiding American foreign policy with the Saudis, the ambassador found them to approach women with less gender bias than senior men here in the United States. We laughed at the irony, but we knew the underlying truth: across the globe, women represent an underappreciated segment. Despite comprising more than half the world's population, women are undervalued. This is why today women represent the largest emerging market in the world.

■ ■ ■

As technological advancements enable companies to cross borders seamlessly and global markets keep check on governance systems, the historical boundaries of geography and political regimes are increasingly disappearing. No longer enough to evaluate a company's country of domicile in today's economy by its political leaders and macro economy, we must also account for its global influences, including sales footprint and global investor base.

An emerging market investor increasingly has to identify novel opportunities, not by countries, but by more fluid and dynamic categorizations. Money would seek the same fundamental characteristics and opportunities: vast markets with productive capacity that have historically been underpenetrated for structural reasons. Like emerging markets, these segments too can thrive with a boost of capital, jolt of technology, and/or modernized institutions.

Through this lens, women represent a vast segment. They have untapped productive capacity, and they have been structurally underrepresented in investor portfolios and broader economies. Put differently, the demographic of "women" shares the fundamental characteristics that have lured emerging market investors for decades.

The catalyst for a repricing is occurring now, driven by the rise of technology, sustainability investing, and evolving norms. Investing in women not only promotes ethics and equality, but also a generous return to our economies and our portfolios.

Vast Segment with Productive Capacity

Leaders in emerging countries have come to understand the importance of women in their economy over the last several years. During dinner with Namibian President Hage Geingob in 2019 during the UN General Assembly, he shared with me his goal of advancing women as a means to doubling his country's productivity, the same theme he touched on during his statement at the general debate.

Before our dinner, he had shared with the gathering of global presidents and prime ministers, "We must bequeath to our children a world that is more peaceful, inclusive and prosperous; a world in which they can access opportunities to employ their gifts and talents; each according to his or her need and each according to his or her ability; a world where women and the youth should no longer suffer exclusion. The future hinges on their participation. And we must ensure that they are no longer on the fringes of decision making but at the forefront of galvanizing multilateral efforts for poverty eradication, quality education, climate action and inclusion."[1]

As *potjiekos* was served and the aromas filled the room, we further discussed the critical topics of the day: global exchange rates, interest rates, and Namibia's goals of universal education to lift its citizens out of poverty. President Geingob came across as a traditional politician, oozing charisma, laughing, and livening the room as he joked throughout the evening, his amiable personality keeping the attention of everyone in the room.

Yet despite his lighthearted demeanor, the conversations throughout the evening kept coming back to his ideas about adding women to government and business until finally he asked if he could have the floor. But rather than taking the spotlight himself, he asked a member of his entourage to come up on stage. A young woman accepted his microphone and began expounding on Namibia's goals for educating women and bringing them up into government and business. Soon after that, Emma Theofelus, at the tender age of 23, became one of Africa's youngest cabinet ministers and one of 100 most influential African women.[2]

President Geingob not only recognized the value that women brought to the economy and his country but led from the top by bringing a woman into his entourage and giving her the opportunity to communicate directly to the most influential emerging market investors in the world. By recognizing her skills and expertise, he demonstrated his belief in the promising future of women and the change they can have in not just his country, but around the globe.

Women have historically been underrepresented in all sectors of the marketplace, from low-wage labor to senior management of major corporations. They've been paid less for the same work, had their ideas cast aside, and struggled to climb the corporate ladder.

Women have the same raw skills as men, the same ability to generate ideas and strategize investments, and trends indicate that they're more willing to bring their ideas to market than ever. As women have become increasingly educated, a new pool of high-caliber talent is entering the labor force. These talented women are bursting with ideas, skill, and energy that bring profits to investors and to their own families. Structural barriers have limited their advancement, but those barriers are rapidly being eroded as today's megathemes take hold.

From cities to nations across the globe, government leaders have recognized the connection between gender parity at work and its potential for massive productivity improvements. Employing women also lifts families out of poverty and creates wealth that can impact families for generations, driving a virtuous cycle of output and prosperity. When Marty Walsh was mayor of Boston, he recognized that his jurisdiction was structurally disadvantaged compared to other major cities given its higher percentage of women. With women underpaid and underrepresented in the workforce, he couldn't compete with the other cities because statistics showed women at such an economic disadvantage. In response, he rolled out a series of programs across the city. I served as a supporter of the Boston Women's Workforce Council, which is committed to closing regional gender and racial pay gaps, and brought my then-firm to become a signatory of the Boston Talent Compact, joining more than 250 companies that committed to equal pay for women. Secretary Walsh's ideas echo a growing sentiment that the advancement of women precipitates the advancement of the larger economy.

Whispers of Opportunity

While Secretary Walsh shined a bright spotlight on the gender disparity in his community, other communities are more muted in their acknowledgment.

While living in India many summers ago, I spent each morning reading the newspaper. As a student of anthropology, the newspaper was a window into the country, a fascinating real-time source of cultural practices, political maneuvers, and personal perspectives.

On the first morning of my newspaper-reading ritual, I found a story tucked in the back pages of the paper. It told of a bride who, rather than enjoying a honeymoon with her new husband days after her wedding, had been burned to death by his family, in her own kitchen, because of the perceived lack of value that her family had provided as a dowry. Her brutal death enabled the husband to marry again and collect a new dowry, without the inconvenience of a divorce or a second wife to support.

I was shocked, but every day I found a story of another bride. The methods of killing were different, but the cause was depressingly similar. A woman's value was based on the dowry her family could provide. For these murderous men, that price was worth more than the life of the woman herself.

These women's lives had been reduced to a few words in a newspaper, and my heart hurt every day as I read their stories. I collected their clippings and carefully curated them in a macabre jewelry box of treasures taken from the world too soon. By the end of the summer, my box was full of stories, literally at least one for each day of my trip. And while I was awash with grief, anger, and disgust, I also became so much more aware when Indian women began rising to leadership positions. During the next two decades, more and more Indian enterprises were placed in the capable hands of well-educated, business-savvy women. While progress is typically gradual, it escalates once it reaches critical mass.

Now move the clock two decades forward. India's $3 trillion economy is led by Nirmala Sitharaman, who has ranked thirty-seventh on the *Forbes* list of the World's 100 Most Powerful Women 2021. A woman was leading the fastest growing economy in the world. Women in India run state governments and serve as CEOs and CFOs of many corporations. The rise of women has led to sweeping changes in its archaic laws. The government now guarantees women equal shares of their parental property. Furthermore, and most important, a woman cannot be discarded without any monetary support by her husband chanting the word *"talaq"* (divorce) three times.

In Western markets, when I interview management teams, I expect to find a man sitting in the CEO seat across from me. However, this isn't the case in every region, and especially not in developing Asia. In China, Vietnam, and India, I'm no longer surprised to meet female CEOs. I've become accustomed to their prevalence. I am grateful for their time and insights, and as they take my questions, I often find myself nodding, appreciating the awkward dichotomy in which they live.

The juxtaposition of these two realities is stark. While much of Asia struggles with the subjugation of women and their rights, they are also leading the way for women in the business world. In Asia, there is more representation of women in CEO positions and boards than in the developed world. Why? Perhaps it is due to the joint family model, which enables availability of childcare. Perhaps it is tied to a deliberate focus on educating girls, given these countries' distorted gender ratios due to the prevalence of female abortion. Perhaps the prevalence of positive role models has shown girls that they can make it to the top of corporations or launch their own successful enterprises. I remember one of my own childhood heroes, Prime Minister Indira Gandhi, the first woman to ever hold this position in India. She was not only an able politician, winning over her strong counterpart men, but she also presided over the creation of Bangladesh when Pakistan tried to militarily subjugate its eastern part. She is an early example of a woman who broke through the glass ceiling, serving as a vision that subsequent generations have embraced.

While boardrooms in countries such as the United States have lagged behind in gender equality, countries such as Hong Kong, boasting a 33% rate of women in the boardroom, and China, with 38% of senior executive positions held by women, are leading the way.[3] Women form 41% of CEOs in banking and financial-services industries in India. Almost one-third of the IT sector workforce is women. In 2019, women comprised 51% of all medical school students in India.

China's one-child policy is another example of the striking contrast between subjugation and representation. Due to cultural norms, boys were regarded as more desirable than girls. The government limit on children meant that female children were often sent to orphanages, abandoned, aborted, or even trafficked because of their perceived inability to provide honor, support, and a legacy for their families.

An unintended but welcome consequence of these laws was a new concentration on education of children. Whether they were boys or girls, families put both financial and social support into schooling, in part because they knew that parents or even grandparents might one day need to rely on the financial support of these children.[4] Delaying the birth of their first, and only, child also encouraged women to pursue higher education.[5]

Now, with a shortage of females of marriageable age permeating China, women are taking advantage of the opportunities for education and furthering their careers, while China scrambles to increase its plummeting birth rate by changing the one-child policy to a two-child policy, and further shifting to a three-child policy only five years later.[6] Perhaps as China recognizes the value of females in corporate leadership and their ability to provide for their families, we will see a further shift in a cultural model where girls are equally as important as boys.

Untapped Potential

The nearby countries of the Gulf Cooperation Council (GCC) have enacted changes in women's rights as well. While few would argue that gender norms in the GCC meet Western standards, the pace of liberalization in the Middle East lately has been startling. Saudi Arabia recently jumped more points on the World Bank's Women and Business ranking than any other country has in history, fueled by a raft of measures that give women unprecedented economic freedoms. Reforms range from the practical, such as enabling women to be a head of household, to the arcane, such as removing the obedience provision. These reforms power economic growth by encouraging productivity from 50% of their population, fueling their nation's output and doubling their GDP.

It doesn't seem that long ago that I was a recent college graduate accompanying my father on a business trip in nearby Kuwait. Our host invited a group of us to join him for a boat ride in the gorgeous Persian Gulf. A warm breeze riffled my hair as I watched the stunning city skyline grow smaller, and I felt the weight of the country's oppressive cultural expectations lift from my shoulders into the bright sky and fresh breeze of the ocean.

Soon a police boat approached us. Four men came aboard, and their voices and gestures grew more aggressive as they pointed at me and shouted in Arabic. They demanded our passports, which we quickly surrendered, and began making phone calls after scrutinizing the documents. The situation grew so tense I wondered if we would be arrested, though I couldn't understand what we had done wrong. Several wrought minutes later, they were assuaged and stepped back onto their own boat, speeding away nearly as quickly as they arrived.

Our host apologetically turned to my father and me to explain the reason we were stopped. The police had spotted me, a single young woman, on a boat full of men, and they wanted to know what I was doing there. They had been on the phone confirming my relationship to my father.

Compare that episode to an evolution 13 years later. In 2020, one of Fortune 500's most powerful women in the world, Rania Nashar, led Saudi Arabia's Samba Financial Group to $2 billion in operating income in nine months—in the middle of a pandemic.[7]

The world is waking up to women's abilities in all areas of the work-force and their capabilities to guide companies well and make innovative decisions to lead their companies to higher performance. I'm often struck by how much progress we've made, especially when I hear startling statistics like this. Here in the United States, women were only allowed to wear pants on the Senate floor beginning in 1993.

Yet I am not entirely surprised. Within the next decade I was a personal witness to women's progress from the ground up. The approaches to supporting women entering the workforce are varied, but one often overlooked aspect is simply their ability to access the capital they need to pursue the creation or improvement of their own small business.

Earlier in the book I discussed working in rural northern India for a microfinance organization. We aimed to empower people through micro-finance loans to drive economic development for both communities and individuals, almost entirely women. One striking example showed what happened when a woman not only paid back the loan, but also effected long-term changes in her family and her community.

We worked with a community of weavers who were forced to travel long distances to use a sewing machine. The close-knit community in-cluded a young woman, the mother of two young children who had learned weaving from her own mother. Each day she worked tireless-ly creating shawls, blankets, and other household goods along with her neighbors while their children played at their feet. A few times a year, she and the other weavers would travel to another city to use the warping drum to prepare their looms for weaving.

Her family relied on the income from her weaving to pay for school supplies and food, but the arduous and dangerous walk, combined with travel expenses and fees for the use of the drum, meant that the profits from her woven articles were drastically reduced. She dreaded leaving her children behind, but they were too young to make the journey. Other women in the community helped watch them while she was away. A small loan was all that was needed for the community to purchase a sew-ing machine of their own. With the time and money saved on travel, they were able to spend more time working, stabilize their income, pay back the $20 loan, and better support their families. Meanwhile, the young mother was able to raise her children with dignity—in a home with power and running water—and with the confidence that comes with financial empowerment.

Since the 1970s, microfinance has been a foundational part of em-powering women to better their lives by providing small, low-interest loans that are often used to start small businesses. Eighty percent of the poorest recipients of these loans are females.[8] Not only were women re-cipients of the money, but they also decided to whom money was given. Groups of women created networks of empowerment, giving women the types of social and business ties that gave them the social capital to build their businesses. Some women would refuse to become involved if they had to interact with a man. These all-women groups provided a safe space for even the poorest women, supporting them as they worked to build their dreams.[9]

Why women? Microfinance has focused on women for two reasons: one, women often do not have access to the same capital as men, making them ideal candidates for these small-scale projects. Two, women are more likely to repay their loans than men, making them a good investment risk from the lenders' perspective. A study comparing both matriarchal and patriarchal societies found that "women, relative to men, display a greater willingness to repay their loans in both communities irrespective of the type of loan (i.e., individual or group).... In other words, women appear to be naturally better credit risks than men."[10]

Despite this proven loan-repayment track record over decades and across regions, women-led companies receive less funding than their male counterparts on average in both the emerging markets and the developed. To this end, women learn to be capital efficient and maximize the use of every dollar, leaning into their experience to make their companies suc-cessful despite their financial disadvantage. In the United States in 2019, women received a token 2.8% of start-up funding, their all-time high.[11] Yet despite this enormous gap in funding, start-ups founded by women gathered 10% more in cumulative revenue over a five-year period, ac-cording to the Boston Consulting Group. Venture-backed private tech-nology companies founded by women achieve 12% higher revenue than those started by men, and in a study of more than 350 start-ups, businesses founded by women delivered more than twice as much revenue per dol-lar invested than those founded by men.[12]

If emerging economies were to welcome more women into the workforce, they could grow tremendously. According to World Bank, women's unequal representation and unequal pay results in $160 billion being left on the table globally.[13]

When women lead businesses, start their own companies, or work alongside men on boards, they aren't just climbing higher on the corporate ladder. They are bringing wealth to their employers and employees— and to their investors.

The data prove it. No matter where the company is located, businesses with more women in leadership positions outperform those with fewer. Data from countries across the world showed that, since 2012, shares of companies with at least 20% female management outperformed, by 5% on average, those with 15% or less female management.[14] The results were not only statistically significant, but that increase in performance remained steady for almost every year since 2010. This trend was visible across entire industries: where women are more prevalent in leadership, those industries outperform their counterparts.[15] For instance, healthcare, consumer staples, and the communications industry all boasted female board management of more than 20%, and they showed better returns and less volatility for investors.

The benefits of women entering the workforce is not limited to emerging markets or impoverished economies. Investment returns brought by women aren't bound by geographic or economical boundaries. In London, companies with women in more than one out of three executive seats return 10 times the profit than companies with fewer women.[16] In Mexico, despite women receiving 50% less investments than men, they achieve 20% higher revenues than their male peers.[17] Across Asia, boards with more than 30% female members return an average 6.2% on equity, compared to 4.2% for those without female representatives.[18]

While a representation gap remains, we can see striking economic opportunities for change and progress. If women and men played identical roles in the labor market, the global economy could see a boost of $28 trillion, a 26% increase.[19] While the numbers vary from market to market, the figures are eye-popping. China's GDP could increase by 20%, or $4.2 trillion; Brazil's could increase by 30%, or $853 billion; and India's could increase an astounding 60%, or $2.9 trillion. The figures are even greater in the developed world: 26% for the United Kingdom ($989 billion), 19% for the United States ($4.3 trillion), and 19% for France ($618 billion). Supporting half of a nation's population to enter the workforce at the same rate as men has the potential to add, quite literally, trillions of dollars to a country's economy.

While statistics from around the world prove that including women is good for businesses and investors, why is there such disparate representation?

Structural Barriers

One of my first trips abroad was a vacation to Thailand with my parents. On a gorgeous island known for scuba diving and beautiful beaches, I remember being enamored with the bright colors in the market as silk weavers presented me silkworms on a platter, literally spewing delicate silk before my eyes. Food vendors carved fresh watermelon into elaborate flower designs, and beautiful stupas rose in a stunning background. At only five years of age, I had the honor of meeting Prime Minister Prem Tinsulanonda, who would later go on to sign the UN Convention on the Elimination of All Forms of Discrimination Against Women (CEDAW) in 1985. The signing of CEDAW was a major step for women's rights in Thailand, though there is still much work to be done. CEDAW has been credited with several policy and law changes, including allowing women the right to choose their surnames after marriage, improving the criminal justice system to protect women accused of crimes, and providing harsher penalties for men found guilty of rape, including marital rape.[20]

Since the airport at Bangkok is a hub in cross-Asia travels, I have passed through the city many times. Despite happy memories of pristine beaches of Koh Phi Phi, scuba diving among lionfish, the jungles of the north, and the tantalizing but oh-so-spicy food, and the rich, multifaceted culture, the image that lives with me is the forlorn face of a young teenager.

Waiting in line for a concierge to find out my departure gate, my eyes met those of a girl dressed in a T-shirt and jeans. Her small, adolescent frame was dwarfed by her traveling companion, a stout, balding, confident man in his 60s, standing protectively close to her. When her gaze caught mine, the sadness in her eyes was palpable. I couldn't help but wonder what she was doing here, in the airport, with this white man old enough to be her grandfather. While I tried to believe their relationship was aboveboard, the contrast was too great. One of the horrific realities for many girls across the globe is the sex trade. And while it's a problem in every country, Bangkok is known for its exploitation of women. I still think about that downhearted girl sometimes. *Where is she now? Is she even still alive?*

Women are less likely to work outside the home at all and when they do, it's more likely to be part time. They're also less likely to advance into management, and on average they earn 15% less than men in the same roles.[21]

Women's representation in the workplace decreases as they climb the rungs of the corporate ladder, and these statistics remain unchanged across the employment spectrum. For example, in large companies surveyed globally, 130 out of 3,000, or 4.3%, have women CEOs.[22] Only 4.2% of companies in Latin America and the Caribbean have women CEOs. Nor is the United States immune to this male-dominated corporate culture. Its large corporations have fewer women CEOs than there are male CEOs named John. A mere 4.1% of them have a woman at the helm, and women make up only 15% of board members and other executive positions.[23]

Beneath the statistics lie unspoken structural barriers that women face in the workforce worldwide. These occur throughout critical stages of development, from youth to adulthood. Starting with the most restrictive countries, access to equal education prevents girls from reaching their full potential in the workplace. When faced with the financial decision to choose which children to educate, parents in poverty invariably favor their sons over their daughters.[24] Even if this barrier is overcome, obstacles ranging from household chores to gender-based violence can bring girls' education to an abrupt halt when they're needed at home or too embarrassed, too uncomfortable, or too unsafe to return to school. In addition, menstruation is a further barrier hindering education for girls. Some cultures require females to isolate during menstruation, causing shame and barring girls from participating in school. But even if isolation isn't required, difficulties with sanitation and access to menstrual supplies can force girls to drop out of school altogether.

In established markets, such as the United States, gender bias plays a role in the fields girls are steered toward and how they are expected to behave in school. Girls are often guided away from higher-paying STEM fields, even though they are just as capable, and they are pushed toward more gender-normative (and often lower-paying) roles, such as those of teachers.[25]

Finally, reflecting on the girl in Thailand, the flourishing sex trade invariably targets young females, preventing them from education and keeping them from learning skills that would provide the opportunity for different employment.

Sex slavery, however, is only an extreme example of many more common barriers. When girls become adults, they're faced with two new sets of hurdles. These are pronounced in nearly all societies and cultures around the world. First, the weight of domestic norms and expectations has been a difficult burden to shed. On average, women complete 2.5 times more unpaid care and household work than men. In some markets, such as Asia and the Pacific, this number reaches as high as four times the amount of time.[26] Women in poorer societies spend a collective 200 million hours each year simply gathering water for their households. These demands on women's time leave fewer hours to dedicate to work, further education, and learning new skills, resulting in lower overall workplace participation.

Second, unequal pay continues to plague women despite the attention from media and political figures. Across the developed and emerging world, even when women work the same number of hours, their pay is not commensurate with men's, particularly when motherhood is accounted for. After birthing her first child, a woman's hourly pay rate compared to a man's declines steadily, finally peaking at a 33% difference on average. While women in developed countries have been delaying the age they take on parenthood—and thus delaying the beginning of this growing wage gap—this delay has not been mirrored in other regions.[27] Ivanka Trump, one of my peers at Wharton, stated in her speech at the 2016 Republican National Convention, "As researchers have noted, gender is no longer the factor creating the greatest wage discrepancy in this country; motherhood is." Though I disagree that gender is no longer a factor, motherhood clearly has become an even larger factor in unequal wages.

Given the benefits to society, the opportunity costs of leaving those cherubic faces at home, and the work ethic of women, I often wonder why mothers' salaries are paid at a discount to men's. Really, why don't they earn a premium instead?

Equally unfortunate, a woman's childbearing years align perfectly with the optimal years for launching a career. The mid-20s and the

30s are intense years in life, both personally and professionally. If women had designed the system, especially given their longer life spans, would there be ample second careers? Would careers peak later to preserve those years for family?

In some cultures, the role of women is so constrained to childbirth and rearing that even visitors are subjected to comments. After my college graduation, I spent time in Maceio, Brazil. I have noted earlier that I was stunned to see that, due to a combination of the sun's bronzing effect and the mixing of races, everyone appeared the same: black, white, and every color in between. I couldn't sense racial discrimination, a refreshing and inspiring change. But gender inequality was palpable.

When my host family picked me up from the airport, instead of the typical discussions of strangers meeting for the first time, the mother exclaimed, "My, your hips are so narrow! How can you ever bear children?" My educational achievements and training were unimportant to her when compared to the ultimate purpose of my life: the responsibility to bear children.

Beyond the familial and household burdens women face, their entry into the workforce are limited by the historical and cultural norms that require women to prioritize caring for their families and their households. In South America, while men often serve as waiters in restaurants and staff at hotels, women are much more likely to be out at the market, hustling to sell goods they've grown or created. Their work to provide for their families through any means possible shows innovation and persistence, but their limited representation in the workplace also shows a lack of understanding from business owners of women's abilities to work in a steady job.

In contrast, as women have increasingly entered the workforce in Latin America, their income has lifted a startling 30% of households out of extreme poverty in a 10-year period.[28] These implications underscore the value of women working outside the home, not to mention that such a massive shift happened in only a single decade. Imagine what could happen if women were increasingly welcomed into the workforce.

Why Now?

Whenever I've been abroad, but especially on my travels to more conservative regions, I've been aware of standing out, even in a sea of humanity in bustling urban areas. While I don't wear traditional Indian dress, I do conform to the social norms of wearing conservative clothing. But no matter how much I conform on the outside, I feel the weight of the eyes on me, viewing me as an outsider despite my best attempts at fitting into the culture.

Standing out as a light-skinned, jeans-wearing, free-smiling young woman in Indonesia was good practice for being a professional woman in attending a Chartered Financial Analyst (CFA) Society meeting in Boston. As the only woman in a room full of men, every move and every word was scrutinized by my male peers. Nearly two decades later, I marvel at the progress made as I sit on the Board of the CFA Society Boston. One of our strategic goals is bringing more diverse faces into the industry, including like-minded women who see the value in the ideas women bring to the table.

The future is now.

As investors seek novel markets to deploy capital, women represent tremendous potential. In the United States alone, women hold a majority of wealth, represent nearly half of our country's millionaires, and are set to inherit 70% of the $40 trillion that will transfer over the next 40 years. The investments made in women over the past two decades include several major fields: education, workplace policies that promote gender equality, and an increasing focus on equitable healthcare. These policies, which ultimately break the glass ceiling and allow women to reach their full potential, are coming to fruition.

Though we are far from gender parity in education worldwide, major progress has been made. Since 1995, 180 million more girls have enrolled in primary and secondary school, and the number of girls enrolled in tertiary school has tripled from 38 million to 116 million between 1995 and 2018. Girls also tend to outperform boys in reading and equal them in mathematics in most countries.[29] In the United States, women are 24.7% more likely to enroll in higher education than men and earn 57% of all bachelor's degrees.[30]

They are not only highly educated but entrepreneurial too. Women represent more than twice the number of annual start-up founders, and they are increasingly likely to become serial entrepreneurs. One study of 400 entrepreneurs showed that while 18% of males planned to begin a new business venture in the next three years, nearly half of all women had the same plans.[31] Women are more likely to be first-time home buyers, live six to eight years longer than men on average, and are more likely to be healthier over their lifetime as well.

Yet the gap remains between the investment dollars women receive compared to their male peers. Women are structurally starved for capital. What are the drivers that will create change?

Consumer Capital

One major benefit of globalization is the rise of the consumer class. Among the customers that can jump-start our global GDP, women are the fastest growing consumer demographic across them all. That has led to a parallel phenomenon: women creating business growth via women.

As any MBA student is taught, you have to know your target market. Women are better at targeting women. In today's new economy, women are innovating by developing solutions that benefit their lives and their families: childcare, sustainable beauty and fashion products, and caretaking. Male-run boards and venture capitalists often do not understand the potential of these products, opting instead to back products they are more familiar with.

Wildly successful "unicorns" founded by women are shining examples of what can happen when women receive the funding they need. 23andMe, founded by Anne Wojcicki, is the first of its kind direct-to-consumer genetic testing company. Not only did it have $305 million in revenue in 2020, but it also has provided priceless data helping researchers study Parkinson's disease, obesity, depression, and other disorders tied to genetics.[32] Houzz is a business focused on home remodeling, inspired by founder Adi Tatarko's own struggle in remodeling her family home. Houzz's unique network of contractors and home improvement experts has built a community that garnered Houzz a profit of $500 million in 2020.[33] Jenn Hyman and Jenny Fleiss founded Rent the Runway as college students at Harvard Business School after Jenn watched her sister spend $2,000 on a dress for a wedding. The idea of rentable, affordable fashion was born. Madam C.J. Walker was born in poverty in Delta, Louisiana, to former slaves turned sharecroppers. She became the first self-made "millionairess" and provided gainful work to tens of thousands of people through her innovation: hair products made specifically for black women.[34]

None of these successful businesses would have been possible without the initial investment of financial backers to get the businesses up and running.[35]

Investing in women does more than close the gap. In companies big or small, female leadership drives returns, and investing in them isn't charity. It has the potential to add trillions to the world's economy, reduce the cyclical effect of poverty, and bring innovative ideas we can all benefit from into the marketplace.

Technology

As technology continues to change the way we share ideas, reach our audiences, find funding, and connect with people around the world, women are leveraging that technology to start businesses at a higher rate than ever. Women are increasingly opting for the flexibility of starting their own businesses because the work alternatives they have aren't satisfactory for various reasons. The inspiring Sallie Krawcheck, former C-level executive at two major banks and co-founder and CEO of Ellevest, credits cloud-computing technology and the ability to democratize investing through crowdfunding as two of the main reasons the path to entrepreneurship has never been easier.[36] In my own experience, technology has never been cheaper or more accessible, and it enables founders to readily build competitive businesses that have the potential to disrupt the status quo. Not only is product development further enabled with technology, so is consumer development.

With access to technology, entrepreneurs can build social capital to help launch their businesses and interact with people outside their normal spheres of influence, giving them more opportunities. What's more, technology gives more women the confidence to put their ideas out into the world, free from gender bias. In a study of female entrepreneurs in Saudi Arabia, women noted that they considered the Internet a "safe space" where they can interact with the world outside of gender norms of correct behavior. Participants in the study pointed to gaining independence, proving their abilities to their families, and taking pride in building successful businesses from the ground up as reasons they were driven to this area of entrepreneurship. These benefits, for many women, were more important than the income they earned.[37]

Finally, women are rising as working professionals and social actors, increasingly using technology as a platform to bring their voices to the forefront as they advocate for themselves. Social movements from #MeToo to the continued fight for #PayParity have grown thanks to technology's ability to connect women from across cities and countries, underscoring the importance of social movements and giving a voice to those who may otherwise have gone unheard.

The first programmer in the world was a woman named Ada Lovelace. Today, female robots named "Siri," "Alexa," and "Cortana" have been programmed by men to operate as virtual assistants. Despite the irony, the digitization of the world supercharges the opportunities for women across the globe.

Investment Capital

Diversity, equity, and inclusion programs are bringing more women into the workforce and particularly into finance. One study by the International Finance Corporation, Oliver Wyman, and Rock Creek found that women account for only 8% of senior investment officials in emerging markets and only 10% in developed markets. Nearly 70% of senior investment teams surveyed were composed completely of men.[38] Yet, women- and minority-run firms have been proven to outperform the broader market.[39]

Nothing succeeds like success. Bringing more diversity into our industry will be simple if women and other minorities continue to perform as they have already. The returns of women investment portfolios today exceed those of men–run investment portfolios. The dollars that are allocated are therefore invested in even more likely winners, hence driving the stronger return of women's upstarts than men's. In First Round Capital's portfolio, women-founded companies outperformed men-founded companies by 63%, and a survey of 350 start-ups found that companies founded by women delivered more than twice as much revenue per dollar invested than those founded by men.[40]

Women in investment positions are critical to unlocking the potential economic gains women can bring to the world. My friend and champion Rosie Rios, former US Treasurer, speaks of power centers as the 3-Cs: corporate boards, C-suites (top-level corporate positions such as CEOs, CFOs, and COO), and Congress. When corporate boards and C-suite executives are accountable to their investors, and those investors are focused on sustainable initiatives, women have the opportunity to guide businesses to profitability and growth, from both financial and social positions. As the world has shifted its focus to sustainable and ethical business models, women have naturally risen to lead these changes. Women have seemed to naturally serve in roles such as teachers, nurses, and caretakers, crucial and demanding jobs that are nonetheless often low paying with little room for advancement. Now, in focusing on sustainable investing, women are shifting to caretaking of not just individuals or their own families, but the entire world.

Queens of Wall Street

Via sustainable investing, portfolio managers drive investments in firms with more inclusive representation and benefit from a set of more novel investment opportunities and higher returns. This symbiotic process drives a sustainable global economy, and investment in sustainable business models and green energy are expected to accelerate over the coming years. Investors are beginning to evaluate other factors besides the black-and-white, profit-and-loss standards of their investments. They are looking at how their business model affects the environment, their customers, and employees, and the ethics of how their companies are run. Investors increasingly examine these ESG factors as an important measure of growth potential. The goals are lofty and ambitious—and the investors espousing these virtues are typically women.

In large companies 58% of sustainability executives are female, a remarkably high number compared to the paltry 15% female representation in executive positions overall.[41] The cynic in me wonders if this development is simply greenwashing and tokenism, addressing key challenges in advancing the industry's sustainability objectives while simultaneously claiming gender progressiveness. Indeed, investors can check many boxes by hiring a senior woman to lead ESG. They show both willingness to hire a woman in a visible role and to develop an ESG platform. This prototypical woman, sitting siloed outside of the core investment function, offers lip-speak, saying the right thing and looking pretty but not actually influencing how investments are allocated or creating a structural path for women in the industry. It's become the latest iteration of the "Pink Suite," similar to human resources, where women receive an executive position without the teeth of authority to make sweeping changes.

I have often found myself on ESG panels sitting beside, most typically, other women speaking of ESG's promise. They promise not just corporate profits, but improved working conditions, environmental healing, and the assurance of changes that benefit all of society. I sometimes wonder, does our gender discredit the ESG movement's momentum?

However, the optimist in me looks at the tremendous strides we have made and the power we have accumulated in the pursuit of these ideals. Ultimately, if women are the ones to usher in the new, more responsible era of capitalism, that is a beautiful legacy we might well embrace.

We have the opportunity to change the narrative from the "Kings of Wall Street" to the "Queens and Kings of Wall Street." We can make a lasting impact on the generations of women who follow in our footsteps. I see us driving the advancement of data-science practices in the field of asset management and making thoughtful, responsible decisions backed by data. These decisions impact not just our own businesses, but will also lead the world to invest in ESG more broadly. The industry is in its infancy, and as it gathers momentum, the emerging market of women is gathering momentum right alongside it. Women can leave a legacy in leading this generation of investors into impactful, profitable investments that will shape the future into a place where women's innovations are welcome in the marketplace, their ideas in business are sought after, and they are valued for the perspectives, experience, and education they bring to the table.

Each step women take in executive boardrooms, investment portfolios, and capitol chambers echoes down the halls as the momentum of change builds to the coming crescendo. The swelling music foreshadows the transformation that can happen when women take their places in leadership, places that are imperative to continued growth in all aspects of our society. Individuals, corporations, and political leaders from around the world are in agreement: now is the time to invest in women.

In 2020, I celebrated these observations with friend and champion Amanda Pullinger, longtime CEO of 100 Women in Finance. We embraced our femininity, first with fittings of Royal jewelry in the Cayman Islands and weeks later at a jubilee at Buckingham Palace.

Three hundred and fifty women from around the world gathered to celebrate both the success we had found and the futures we were chasing. As we walked up the red-carpeted Grand Staircase, the contrast of the intricate bronze castings, paintings of past royalty, and vaulted ceilings reminded me of just how far we had come.

We may have been dressed like princesses, but there was no doubt that the future held a place for us as queens, a different kind of royalty, galvanized by mettle and determination, gumption, and grit. We joined the royal family in toasting the next generation of Wall Street, today's women. Together, we have the potential to not only benefit from the next generation of investments, we will drive it.

Conclusion

On the morning of November 9, 2016, I visited the coffee shop in my seaside town with my young son, Griffen. As he peered at the scrumptious pastries through the bakery window, his eyes settled in on a supersized chocolate chip cookie. *Good choice*, I thought, and I obliged. I was in a mood to splurge. We were celebrating his third birthday, and I was suffering from mom guilt. I would be flying down shortly to New York, missing my son's big day. Later that evening, I was scheduled to meet with António Guterres, the incoming Secretary General of the United Nations.

Griffen and I sat along the sea, with the cool Boston air and the low-lying cloud cover—him with his cookie and me with a warm cup of minty black tea.

This was no ordinary day. Hours later, I touched down in Manhattan. A dense fog hung over the buildings, and the city was gray. As I walked the streets, the hustle of New York endured, but an eerie stillness hung in the air. A soft drizzle dimmed the city lights, and the sounds of the streets were seemingly muted.

The night before, the election of Donald J. Trump as US president had been announced. The city was stunned. While I was a frequent traveler to the city, this day felt as ghostly as another I had experienced before—9/11.

Gripping my umbrella, I made my way to the address I had been given, a nondescript restaurant bar in SoHo. Inside, men and women sipped on glasses of wine as they spoke in a hush. "Did you anticipate last night's outcome?" one incredulously whispered, while another responded, "How did this happen?"

Moments later, our dinner guest was introduced. The incoming Secretary-General of the UN greeted us with brief remarks, somber and likely shaken by the unusual circumstances. After his short speech,

I made my way to greet him. When we shook hands, I was captivated by his kind smile and gentle demeanor. Despite the formality in our roles, I inquired, "What do you make of last night's news?"

Guterres seemed bewildered. Nevertheless, he shared his interpretation, apolitical and poignant, of the events. Coming from a decade as the UN High Commissioner for Refugees, he had seen his share of uprisings before. "People clamor for a voice," he explained. He referenced his experience with the Syrian migrant crisis firsthand. His view was that the crisis began with farmers who were clamoring to be heard. Mass protests began in 2011 in Daraa, a drought-stricken province. Agrarian protestors of all ages took to the street to demonstrate for political and economic reforms. Following the arrest and alleged torture of a group of children, their clamors no longer went unheard. Protests ensued across the country, including in the capital Damascus, setting in motion one of the largest human crises in recent history.

Guterres expanded his remarks to address the topic of our meeting that evening—investing in a geopolitically uncertain world. While we as investors yearned to listen, he explained, the people yearned to speak. Peace and prosperity can never be achieved in the emerging or developed markets until each voice is lifted.

His comments matched the way I felt about the rise of people and the role of technology in giving them voice. Guterres and I spoke of social media's role in aggregating the voice of the silenced and bringing their views to the forefront. From my own work, I knew that the possibilities were endless. I wondered how he would prioritize our earth's opportunities and challenges.

Our conversation soon shifted from regional risks to opportunities for economic growth. I wanted to know how he could enact his vision, and I pressed, "What are your priorities in this new role?"

His answer surprised me. He said that there were two—of equal importance. One was pragmatic. A critical priority was engaging the support of the United States, a charter member country, the host of the UN headquarters, and the greatest contributor of financial capital. That made sense to me. The other, he said, was equally ambitious: climate change. It is the greatest looming disaster facing our planet, he relayed, the cause of the European migrant crisis. His view was that it was time for our globe's leaders, governmental and corporate, to take decisive action.

As his words became more impassioned, a group swelled around us. Investors began taking notes, asking questions, and looking for more.

As their voices began to fill the space, I felt my worlds fusing together: I had run sustainable strategies for over a decade, and I ran emerging market funds as well. The notions of sustainability and emerging markets were becoming one.

Fellow Travelers

As a portfolio manager held to standards of impact and sustainability, my work with the United Nations has progressed. I was later invited to join an expert working group at the United Nations on the Sustainable Development Goals. The interdisciplinary group comprised a range of leading professionals, from nongovernmental organizations (NGOs) to investors to technologists. In turn, we each spoke with practitioner knowledge about our institutional commitments and vision. Having been an early signatory to responsible principles, the first for a quantitative investment manager, I offered views on data-driven solutions. After hearing us all, our host, Mathieu Verougstraete, a Development Finance Expert at the United Nations, asked us to pause.

Mathieu broke the silence with a profound question: "For all the assets invested with a sustainability mandate, why is there so little impact?"

His question prompted a deep inward look. *How can investment capital, held to high standards of returns, drive social impact?*

The reason the question needs to be asked is because we have reached a historic convergence of development finance and private finance. The private sector increasingly works alongside development banks on innovative financing strategies. These worlds were previously separate, but now development finance institutions, including the International Finance Corporation (IFC), the Inter-American Development Bank (IDB), and the US International Development Finance Corporation (DFC), have the opportunity to shift risk capital to impact capital.

However, the alignment of economic growth with social development is not a new concept. Economic stability provides social opportunity. My own life story reflects this. My father grew up without electricity or transportation and, sometimes, without shelter. My mother grew up in New York City. Her parents, Jews who had escaped the Holocaust, arrived in Ellis Island from war-torn Europe. With nearly nothing in their pockets to start, my families worked their way up from poverty; both my parents were immigrant refugees, and they became research physicians. For them, the pathway out of poverty was education. That enabled my parents to achieve medical degrees and raise a family with a comfortable lifestyle. With stability came the ability to build assets that enabled them to invest in their children and further grow their wealth for generations beyond. Breaking the chain of generational poverty, both within families and within societies, is ultimately enabled through access to capital and asset building.

What's new, then, is not the alignment itself, but the transformational opportunity for private sector capital to accelerate economic development. Private sector capital consists of assets from endowments, foundations, pension funds, and individuals. The wealth from this base multiples the capital that the public sector can offer. The tectonic shifts of our era—technology advancements and sustainability pressures—open a pathway for both traditional investors and the communities in which they invest. While developed regions are limited in their ability to grow, given their large present base of wealth, emerging markets are uniquely positioned. For these countries, representing 75% of the world's land mass and 80% of the world's people, "sustainable growth" is not an oxymoron but rather a profound opportunity to deliver both alpha and impact.

The road is steep and long, and the end goal may still not be a world with wealth equally distributed and communities without conflict. Human evolution of demands and quests for innovation naturally engenders tension. A Nigerian friend once asked me, "Do you foresee an outcome where the poorest among our poor live at the same standards of the Dangotes?" as she referenced the family of a cement magnate. While differences will remain, pockets of the emerging world show us that it is reasonable to imagine a world in which the poor live with dignity and basic needs are met.

The emerging markets have come to the forefront over the two decades due to varying trends. One was the economic liberalization beginning in the 1990s. The 1995 founding of the World Trade Organization (WTO) resulted in a rise in globalization and a breakdown of global barriers. Trade agreements across countries became more frequent and secure, and it became easier to do business across borders.

While the WTO offered a formal structure for global trade, multilateral institutions advanced their own development playbooks. Some markets drew on the lessons of the past. The painful experiences of Latin

America and Asia in the 1990s taught policy makers in those regions the importance of floating exchange rates, open markets, and sustainable fiscal and debt policies. At the same time, such development agencies as the World Bank, which once focused on institutions, governance, and development programs, became increasingly sophisticated and more effective than they had been even 10 years before.

Perhaps most important, information technology has propelled dramatic international growth. We live in the Information Age. Seamless communication across borders privileges emerging markets, moving them to the forefront. That transition has had a significant impact on my own work. My records were barely digitized at the beginning of the aughts. Just 10 years later, I could email a Nigerian trader in real time about a trade or call a Sri Lankan broker on his mobile phone. (Although with the difference in time zones, he may have preferred not to take my call at nine o'clock in the evening.)

Both of these paths enabled growth and magnified its potential. Emerging markets have benefited from improved institutions, technology, and most tangibly, capital.

Money Changes Everything

Today's emerging markets bear limited resemblance to yesterday's markets. The boom-bust cycles of the twentieth century have been replaced with sophisticated central bank policies and diversified industry bases. The growing middle class and domestic demand fuel their markets, replacing the dependence on commodities in earlier decades. While crony governments remain, today's largest and most promising markets are girded with governance structures that are built both to last and to participate in global economic flows. Today's markets are not rounding errors in investors' allocations but, rather, represent a mainstream investment allocation. Finally, today's markets hold critical geopolitical importance, representing more than half of the constituents of the G20, the intergovernmental forum that addresses major issues related to the global economy, such as international financial stability, climate change mitigation, and sustainable development.

With capital increasingly invested in local technology, emerging markets are positioned for disruption in the decade ahead. The digital revolution is already as advanced in these economies as it is in developed ones. Of the top nations generating revenue from digital services, the majority is in the emerging world.[1] Since 2017, digital revenue in emerging countries has grown by an average of 26% per year compared with 11% in developed countries. Assessed by this metric, Indonesia will soon be more advanced than France or Canada.

Emerging economies have many advantages in technology relative to the developed markets. First, emerging nations are adopting cutting-edge technology at a lower cost, allowing them to fuel domestic demand and overcome traditional obstacles to growth. As evidence, over the past decade, the number of smartphone owners has skyrocketed from 150 million to 4 billion worldwide. More than half the world's population now carry the power of a supercomputer in their pockets.

In addition, emerging economies have demographics on their side. Around 90% of the world's population under 30 live in developing economies.[2] This young cohort is quick to adapt to technology and, often enough, eager to develop it further. As necessity is the mother of invention, the innovations in this historically poor region are vast. The FinTech and telecom revolutions enabled the rise of new, innovative types of savings accounts, credit lending, and other financial tools. These, in turn, fire up entrepreneurs, accelerate businesses, and propel countries toward growth.

As emerging economies surge ahead, developed economies look to access not only precious resources and low-wage labor but also increasingly new target consumers and investors. The "trickle down" economic theory that led to growth in these regions has created robust regions that enable wealth today to "trickle up." Our quest for growth not only fuels these markets, their growth enriches developed economies and enhances our asset values.

The emergence of these markets drives both policies and portfolios and creates novel opportunities and risks as new sectors emerge and others die. These changing demographics are quite literally shaping tomorrow's ecosystem.

In a capitalist system often vilified for achieving growth through the commodification of humans, the emerging markets offer us an opportunity to reimagine capitalism. While the West's capitalist model was built on the backs of exploited labor, a more global approach that systemically arbitrages costs and broadens opportunities creates a thriving system that drives not only economic development but social development as well.

Reimagined Capitalism

Sustainable investing calls on investors to appreciate the dual purpose of their capital: to generate a return for the investor and to use capital to build tomorrow's ecosystem. Investment portfolios are "future fit" when they are invested to drive profitable returns not only today but also a generation ahead. With today's technology and sensibilities, we can build portfolios that reinforce climate mitigation, ensure social stability, and promote strong governance norms.

Never have former UN Secretary General Kofi Annan's words been truer: "Healthy societies and healthy markets go hand in hand." Ultimately, the returns of a sustainable strategy should not place social good at the expense of investment returns. A higher-returning strategy will surely replace a low-return strategy. Rather, in leveraging our capital to build structures, physical and idealistic, that are intentionally stable and regenerative, we reinforce its future value.

This systems-based approach links the sources and uses of investment capital, the role of the private sector in society, and the role of investors in driving positive impact. History has shown our ability to lift billions out of poverty, to accelerate the shift to renewable solutions, and to build a world with more dignity and peace for all.

Today's technology enables us to advance these efforts, scale them, and compound the power of our capital. Examples abound. FinTech banks the unbanked as novel frameworks enable credit referencing. Without a government ID or mortgage, the poor are evaluated today on their Internet searches (for diapers vs. booze). HealthTech medicates the remote, with 5G connecting rural villagers to well-educated physicians dwelling in nearby cities or cities afar—the patient need never know. CleanTech powers the homes of the poor, providing stable electricity on which to run their businesses, comfort to warm their homes, and light to educate their children.

From the Red River Delta of Vietnam to the Niger Delta in Nigeria to the United States' own Louisiana Delta, technology, sustainability, and rapidly emerging populations create pathways for today's investors. While the last two decades brought villagers into the cities, and cities from Delhi to Dubai into the mainstream, the coming years will enable us to reach the remaining poor—from the rickshaw pedaling boy in Bangladesh to the girl in Mali carrying water upon her head for her family to drink.

In accessing capital, these regions provide a global opportunity for us to reach those on that very last mile, drive investment returns, and deliver lasting impact.

Mint and Honey

In that tavern in New York with António Guterres, I connected the link between my narrow world of work and the ecosystem in which I operate. The capital I invest not only requires surrounding infrastructure, it builds tomorrow's infrastructure. Indeed, investable companies include those that create 5G communication platforms, automated and cleaner cars, affordable household products, and solar technologies that bring power to households in remote villages, from remote corners of the Amazon rainforest to the clay dwellings in the Sahara desert. These products address unmet needs and improve lives. As consumers spend capital, the virtuous cycle of innovation advances.

The challenge is not *whether* an investor delivers both returns and impact. Rather, it is *how* they are delivered. All financial capital has impact. What we fund literally builds our systems, so we must determine how we will plan our investments to maximize economic returns.

We are embarking on the next generation of investment strategy. A century ago, investors developed formulas to evaluate an investment's intrinsic value. From that was born the great theories of value-based investing and fundamental analysis. Decades later, portfolio theory was born, wherein academics and practitioners alike promoted the appreciation that investment returns and risks intersect, and one can maximize performance by considering the interaction of various stocks in a portfolio.

Secretary-General Guterres said that investors today benefit from today's energy rich environment, and yet we are likewise tasked to build tomorrow's low-carbon ecosystem. As I sipped on another cup of soothing minty black tea alongside Guterres at the end of this long day, the warmth and aroma brought me back to a similar conclusion many years ago.

On a hot and dusty drive home half a world away, my friend and I had been returning home to Amman, Jordan. He stopped along the road, not far from the Syrian border, to have tea with friends in their small, traditional abode. He ushered me in. Their house was nothing fancy. It had clay walls, small windows, and a few firm pillows on which to sit. Our host boiled water, infused with sugar and loose tea leaves, in a kettle over an actual fire. She topped the tea with sprigs of mint and a spoonful of honey.

We sat together in the firelight, sipping the tea, and catching up on our lives. I felt then that I had gone back in time, and it was beautiful.

Hospitality, warmth, love among strangers—these values are at the bedrock of so many emerging cultures. They will have to serve all of us in good stead as we rocket ahead into a perilous twenty-first century.

Someday soon, the power of capital will reach down even to that remote home. Who knows? Maybe that is where the next innovation will begin.

Notes

Introduction

1 World Bank, Gross Domestic Product in 2010 US dollars.
2 "How Is Technology Transforming Global Emerging Markets?," Nomura, April 2018, https://www.nomuraconnects.com/focused-thinking-posts/how-will-technology-transform-global-emerging-markets/.
3 Ruchir Sharma, "Technology Will Save Emerging Markets from Sluggish Growth," *Financial Times*, April 11, 2021, https://www.ft.com/content/2356928b-d909-4a1d-b108-7b60983e3d22.

Chapter 1

1 Domestic shares are shares that are denominated in Renminbi (the official Chinese currency) and traded in the Shanghai and Shenzhen stock exchanges.
2 "Fan Gang—Trade War and China's New Phase of Development," Lecture, Fairbank Center for Chinese Studies, Harvard University, https://fairbank.fas.harvard.edu/events/critical-issues-confronting-china-lecture-series-2-2018-11-07/.
3 Benedict Rogers, "The Nightmare of Human Organ Harvesting in China," *Wall Street Journal*, February 5, 2019.

Chapter 2

1 "Viet Nam Breaks into High Human Development Category Group: UNDP New Report," UNDP in Viet Nam, December 16, 2020.
2 Oxford Business Group, "The Report: Vietnam 2017," https://oxfordbusinessgroup.com/vietnam-2017.
3 Huang Giang, "Talk with Asia's Most Powerful Businesswoman," VietNamNet, March 25, 2012, http://english.vietnamnet.vn/fms/special-reports/20130/talk-with-asia-s-most-powerful-businesswoman.html.

4 Reuters staff, "Samsung Electronics to expand production in Vietnam," Reuters, https://www.reuters.com/article/us-samsung-elec-vietnam-idUSKBN1HR1SD.

5 Stephanie Davis et al., "e-Conomy SEA 2019: Swipe Up and to the right: Southeast Asia's $100 Billion Internet Economy," Think with Google (blog), October 2019, https://www.thinkwithgoogle.com/intl/en-apac/consumer-insights/consumer-trends/e-conomy-sea-2019-swipe-up-and-to-the-right-southeast-asias-100-billion-internet-economy/.

6 "China: Vietnamese Vessels Rammed Its Ships More Than 1,000 Times," CNBC, June 9, 2014, https://www.cnbc.com/2014/06/09/china-vietnamese-vessels-rammed-its-ships-more-than-1000-times.html.

7 "Vietnam States Its Case Ahead of Crucial Climate Convention," *Vietnam Investment Review*, October 27, 2021, https://vir.com.vn/vietnam-states-its-case-ahead-of-crucial-climate-convention-88723.html.

Chapter 3

1 Oilprice.com, "Oil Is Now More Volatile Than Bitcoin," Financial Trend Forecaster, February 27, 2020, https://fintrend.com/2020/02/27/oil-is-now-more-volatile-than-bitcoin/.

2 Raymond J. Kopp, "Replacing Oil: Alternative Fuels and Technologies," *Resources*, November 16, 2006, https://www.resources.org/archives/replacing-oil-alternative-fuels-and-technologies/#:~:text=%20Replacing%20Oil%3A%20Alternative%20Fuels%20and%20Technologies%20,often%20a%20combination%20of%20sticks%20and...%20More%20.

3 Evaldo Costa, "The Future of Electric Vehicles in Brazil," *Behavioural and Social Sciences at Nature Research*, October 12, 2020, https://socialsciences.nature.com/posts/the-future-of-electric-vehicles-in-brazil.

4 "Electric Car Use by Country," Wikipedia, June 2020, https://en.wikipedia.org/wiki/Electric_car_use_by_country.

5 Emirates Media Centre, "Aviation to Contribute $53.1 Billion to Dubai's Economy, 37.5% to Its GDP and Will Support Over 750,000 jobs by 2020," Emirates, November 17, 2014, https://www.emirates.com/media-centre/aviation-to-contribute-531-billion-to-dubais-economy-375-to-its-gdp-and-will-support-over-750000-jobs-by-2020#:~:text=Using%20industry%20growth%20forecasts%20and%20modelling%20projections%20based,rise%20to%20a%20robust%20%2453.1%20billion%20in%202020.

6   Jeevan Thankappan, "Saudi Smartphone Penetration Exceeds Global Average," Tahawultech.com, December 20, 2017, https://www.tahawultech.com/news/saudi-smartphone-penetration-exceeds-global-average/.

7   "Foreign Direct Investment, Net Inflows (BoP, current US$)," The World Bank, https://data.worldbank.org/indicator/BX.KLT.DINV.CD.WD.

8   IMF Staff, "Global Trade Liberalization and the Developing Countries," International Monetary Fund, January 2008, https://www.imf.org/external/np/exr/ib/2001/110801.htm.

Chapter 4

1   Omar Ant and Cagan Koc, "Erdogan Renews Rate-Cut Demands as Economy Erodes Support," Bloomberg, June 1, 2021 (updated June 2, 2021), https://www.bloomberg.com/news/articles/2021-06-01/turkish-lira-weakens-past-8-77-to-fresh-record-versus-dollar.

2   "Palace of Parliament," Bucharest, Romania Attractions, Lonely Planet, https://www.lonelyplanet.com/romania/bucharest/attractions/palace-of-parliament/a/poi-sig/419539/360383.

3   Valeriu Lazar, "Update: Former Tourism Minister Elena Udrea—Sentenced To Six Years in Jail," *Romania Journal*, March 28, 2017, https://www.romaniajournal.ro/society-people/update-former-tourism-minister-elena-udrea-sentenced-to-six-years-in-jail/.

4   Kit Gillet and Marc Santora, "Voters in Romania Reject Years of Scandals and Chaos," *New York Times*, November 25, 2019, https://www.nytimes.com/2019/11/24/world/europe/romania-election.html.

5   Published in 2018 as part of the UN 2030 Agenda for Sustainable Development.

6   The importance of property rights as a source of economic freedom can be seen in the stark contrast between Romania, where private property rights are protected under the law, and South Africa, where the president pushed land reclamation postapartheid and sent markets crashing.

7   "Human Development Index (HDI)," Human Development Reports, United Nations Development Programme, https://hdr.undp.org/en/content/human-development-index-hdi.

8   Andrei Chirileasa, "Romania Becomes Emerging Market—Fin. Min: We Are One Click Away from Billions Looking to Be Invested," *Romania Insider*, https://www.romania-insider.com/romania-bucharest-stock-exchange-emerging-market-september-2020.

Chapter 5

1   Local regulators had shut the market during a particularly volatile period. This is a no-no for institutional investors who need to be able to sell securities on demand.

2   Anchal Vohra, "The Pointlessness of America's Sanctions on Syria's Bashar al-Assad," FP, January 11, 2022, https://foreignpolicy.com/2022/01/11/syria-sanctions-americabiden-europe-economy/.

3   Desmond Tutu, "Divesting From Injustice," HuffPost, https://www.huffpost.com/entry/divesting-from-injustice_b_534994.

4   Desmond Tutu, "We fought apartheid. Now climate change is our global enemy," The Guardian, https://www.theguardian.com/commentis-free/2014/sep/21/desmond-tutu-climate-change-is-the-global-enemy.

5   Caitlin E. Werrell and Francesco Femia, eds., The Arab Spring and Climate Change (Center for American Progress, 2013), https://www.american progress.org/wp-content/uploads/2013/02/ClimateChangeArabSpring.pdf.

Chapter 6

1. "Bara Imambara, Lucknow, India," Atlas Obscura, https://www.atlas obscura.com/places/bara-imambara.

2   "The Legacy of Indian Migration to European Colonies," The Economist, September 2, 2017, https://www.economist.com/international/2017/09/02/the-legacy-of-indian-migration-to-european-colonies.

3   "India Population (live)," Worldometer, https://www.worldometers.info/world-population/india-population/.

4   Shilpa Jamkhandikar, "In Mumbai's Slums, Over Half of Population Probably Infected with Coronavirus, Survey Says," Reuters, July 29, 2020, https://www.reuters.com/article/us-health-coronavirus-india-idINKCN 24U1UL.

5   Shahidur R. Khandker and Hussain A. Samad, "Microfinance Growth and Poverty Reduction in Bangladesh: What Does the Longitudinal Data Say?," The Bangladesh Development Studies 37, nos. 1 and 2 (2014): 127–157, https://www.jstor.org/stable/26538550.

6   "Microfinance in Bangladesh Helps Reduce Poverty for Women," Borgen Magazine, September 12, 2016, https://www.borgenmagazine.com/microfinance-in-bangladesh/.

7   Davidnder K. Madaan, "India's New Economic Policy—A Macro Study," Indian Journal of Asian Affairs 8/9, nos. 1/2 (1995): 104–113, http://www.jstor.org/stable/41950393.

8 Hillary Mayell, "India's 'Untouchables' Face Violence, Discrimination," *National Geographic*, June 2, 2003, https://www.nationalgeographic.com/pages/article/indias-untouchables-face-violence-discrimination.

9 "Satyam Scam: All You Need to Know about India's Biggest Accounting Fraud Story," *Hindustan Times*, April 9, 2015, https://www.hindustantimes.com/business/satyam-scam-all-you-need-to-know-about-india-s-biggest-accounting-fraud/story-YTfHTZy9K6NvsW8PxIEEYL.htm.

10 D. Parthasarathy, "The Caste of a Scam: A Thousand Satyams in the Making," Kafila, February 13, 2009, https://kafila.online/2009/02/13/the-caste-of-a-scam-a-thousand-satyams-in-the-making/.

11 "A World Overheating," Council on Foreign Relations, October 18, 2021, https://www.cfr.org/article/climate-change-world-overheating-how-countries-adapt-extreme-temperature.

12 Zafar Imran, "Climate Change in the Indian Farmers' Protest," *Le Monde diplomatique*, February 1, 2021, https://mondediplo.com/outsidein/climate-indian-farmers.

13 Sanyukta Kanwal, "Agriculture in India—Statistics & Facts," Statista, February 14, 2022, https://www.statista.com/topics/4868/agricultural-sector-in-india/#:~:text=The%20agriculture%20sector%20is%20one,18%20percent%20to%20India's%20GDP.

14 "Acadian Asset Management Launches the First Actively Managed Emerging Market Fossil Fuel Free Strategy," *Business Wire*, May 23, 2017, https://www.businesswire.com/news/home/20170523005331/en/Acadian-Asset-Management-Launches-Actively-Managed-Emerging.

15 Joanna Slater, "Can India Chart a Low-Carbon Future? The World Might Depend on It," *Washington Post*, June 12, 2020, https://www.washingtonpost.com/climate-solutions/2020/06/12/india-emissions-climate/

16 Ibid.

17 "Circular Economy in India: Rethinking Growth for Long-Term Prosperity," Ellen MacArthur Foundation, 2016, https://ellenmacarthurfoundation.org/circular-economy-in-india.

18 "Nirmala Sitharaman," profile, *Forbes*, https://www.forbes.com/profile/nirmala-sitharaman/?sh=66cb530d7bcd.

19 "Global Innovation Index 2021: Tracking Innovation through the COVID-19 Crisis," World Intellectual Property Organization, 2021, https://www.wipo.int/global_innovation_index/en/2021/.

20 Ashok Lalwani, "This Is How India Can Become the Next Silicon Valley," World Economic Forum, October 2, 2019, https://www.weforum.org/agenda/2019/10/india-technology-development-silicon-valley/.

21 "Millennium Development Goals," Sustainable Development Goals Fund (SDGF), https://www.sdgfund.org/mdgs-sdgs.

Chapter 7

1   "WhatIsM-PESA?,"Vodafone,https://www.vodafone.com/about-vodafone/what-we-do/consumer-products-and-services/m-pesa.

2   "Number of ATMs, ATM Cards, & POS Machines," Central Bank of Kenya,https://www.centralbank.go.ke/national-payments-system/payment-cards/number-of-atms-atm-cards-pos-machines/.

3   N. Ndung'u, *The M-Pesa Technological Revolution for Financial Services in Kenya: A Platform for Financial Inclusion* (Academic Press, 2018), https://doi.org/10.1016/B978-0-12-810441-5.00003-8.

4   William Jack and Tavneet Shuri, "Mobile Money: the Economics of M-Pesa," National Bureau of Economic Research, 2011.

5   Business services can now receive payments using a QR code! This feature was introduced in 2017.

6   Report of the Auditor-General and Financial Statements on Kenya Power and Lighting Company PLC for the year ending in June 30, 2021, http://parliament.go.ke/sites/default/files/2021-11/Report%20of%20the%20Auditor-General%20and%20Financial%20Statements%20on%20Kenya%20Power%20and%20Lighting%20Company%20PLC%20for%20the%20year%20ended%2030th%20June%202021.pdf.

7   Alexander Richter, "ThinkGeoEnergy's Top 10 Geothermal Countries 2020—Installed Power Generation Capacity (MWe)," ThinkGeoEnergy, January 7, 2021, https://www.thinkgeoenergy.com/thinkgeoenergys-top-10-geothermal-countries-2020-installed-power-generation-capacity-mwe/.

8   Katie Painter, "Geothermal Energy in Kenya," *The Borgen Project* (blog), July 20, 2020, https://borgenproject.org/geothermal-energy-in-kenya/.

9   "Access to Electricity (% of Population)—South Africa," The World Bank Data, https://data.worldbank.org/indicator/EG.ELC.ACCS.ZS.

10 "Income Inequality by Country 2022," The World Bank Data, https://worldpopulationreview.com/country-rankings/income-inequality-by-country.

11 "Poverty Headcount Ratio at National Poverty Lines (% of population)," The World Bank Data, https://data.worldbank.org/indicator/SI.POV.NAHC.

12 Bruce Baigrie et al., "Why Eskom Is a Mess and What to Do about It," Alternative Information & Development Centre (AIDC).

13 Ibid.

14 Anton Eberhard et al., "South Africa's REIPPPP: Success Factors and Lessons," World Bank Group, https://www.gsb.uct.ac.za/files/ppiafreport.pdf.

15 Robert Muggah and Katie Hill, "African Cities Will Double in Population by 2020. Here Are 4 Ways to Make Sure They Thrive," World Economic

Forum, June 27, 2018, https://www.weforum.org/agenda/2018/06/Africa-urbanization-cities-double-population-2050-4%20ways-thrive/.

16 Lutz Goedde, Amandla Ooko-Ombaka, and Gillian Pais, "Winning in Africa's Agricultural Market," McKinsey & Company, February 15, 2019, https://www.mckinsey.com/industries/agriculture/our-insights/winning-in-africas-agricultural-market#:~:text=More%20than%2060%20percent%20of%20the%20population%20of,agriculture.%20Yet%2C%20Africa%E2%80%99s%20full%20agricultural%20potential%20remains%20untapped.

17 Lauren Frayer, "In Sri Lanka, China's Building Spree Is Raising Questions about Sovereignty," NPR, December 13, 2019, https://www.npr.org/2019/12/13/784084567/in-sri-lanka-chinas-building-spree-is-raising-questions-about-sovereignty.

18 "How Asians View Each Other," Chapter 4 in "Global Opposition to U.S. Surveillance and Drones, But Limited Harm to America's Image," Pew Research Center, July 14, 2014, https://www.pewresearch.org/global/2014/07/14/chapter-4-how-asians-view-each-other/.

19 Eleanor Abbott, "China in Africa," Council on Foreign Relations, last updated July 12, 2017, https://www.cfr.org/backgrounder/china-africa.

20 W. Gyude Moore, "African Countries Should Stay Loyal to China's Troubled Huawei—Regardless of Trump," Quartz Africa, May 27, 2019, https://qz.com/africa/1629078/africa-will-stay-loyal-to-chinas-huawei-regardless-of-trump/.

21 Daniel Slotta, "Huawei's Revenue by Region 2012–2020," Statista, January 13, 2022, https://www.statista.com/statistics/368509/revenue-of-huawei-by-region/.

22 Karishma Vaswani, "Huawei: The Story of a Controversial Company," BBC, March 6, 2019, https://www.bbc.co.uk/news/resources/idt-sh/Huawei.

23 Carlos Mureithi, "Kenya Becomes the Second African Country to Roll Out 5G," Quartz Africa, April 1, 2021, https://qz.com/africa/1990724/kenya-becomes-the-second-african-country-to-launch-5g/.

24 "'You'll Be Fired If You Refuse': Labor Abuses in Zambia's Chinese State-Owned Copper Mines," Human Rights Watch, November 2011, https://www.hrw.org/sites/default/files/reports/zambia1111ForWebUpload.pdf.

25 "Freedom on the Net 2021: China," Freedom House, 2021, https://freedomhouse.org/country/china/freedom-net/2021.

26 Hofstede Insights, https://www.hofstede-insights.com/country/nigeria/.

27 Chimamanda Adichie, "Nigeria Is Murdering Its Citizens," *New York Times*, October 21, 2020, https://www.nytimes.com/2020/10/21/opinion/sunday/chimamanda-adichie-nigeria-protests.html.

28 Emmanuel Akinwotu, "Out of Control and Rising: Why Bitcoin Has Nigeria's Government in a Panic," *The Guardian*, July 31, 2021, https://www.theguardian.com/technology/2021/jul/31/out-of-control-and-rising-why-bitcoin-has-nigerias-government-in-a-panic.

29   Temitayo Lawal, "Nigeria's Diaspora May Have Switched to Cryptocurrency, as Official Remittances Fall by $6bn," *The Africa Report*, August 19, 2021, https://www.theafricareport.com/115305/nigerias-diaspora-may-have-switched-to-cryptocurrency-as-official-remittances-fall-by-6bn/.

30   "Remittances and Fiat Currency Devaluation Drive Africa's Growing Cryptocurrency Economy, and Big Exchanges Recognize the Opportunity," Chainalysis, September 8, 2020, https://blog.chainalysis.com/reports/africa-cryptocurrency-market-2020.

31   Katharina Buchholz, "These Are the Countries Where Cryptocurrency Use Is Most Common," World Economic Forum, February 18, 2021, https://www.weforum.org/agenda/2021/02/how-common-is-cryptocurrency/.

32   "Bitcoin Trading Volume on Online Exchanges in Various Countries Worldwide in 2020," Statista, https://www.statista.com/statistics/1195753/bitcoin-trading-selected-countries/.

33   "The 2021 Global Crypto Adoption Index: Worldwide Adoption Jumps Over 880% With P2P Platforms Driving Cryptocurrency Usage in Emerging Markets," Chainalysis, October 14, 2021, https://blog.chainalysis.com/reports/2021-global-crypto-adoption-index.

34   David Segal, "Going for Broke in Cryptoland," *New York Times*, August 5, 2021, https://www.nytimes.com/2021/08/05/business/hype-coins-cryptocurrency.html.

35   "Nigeria Launches Its Central Bank Digital Currency eNaira," Central Bank Currencies, October 25, 2021, https://centralbankcurrencies.com/news/nigeria-launches-its-central-bank-digital-currency-enaira/.

Chapter 8

1   "Here's How Rich Pablo Escobar Would Be If He Was Alive Today," *UNILAD*, September 13, 2016, https://www.unilad.co.uk/film/heres-how-rich-pablo-escobar-would-be-if-he-was-alive-today/.

2   "Pablo Emilio Escobar 1949–1993 9 Billion USD—The Business of Crime—5 'Success' Stories," MSN, January 17, 2011.

3   "Decline of the Medellín Cartel and the Rise of the Cali Mafia," U.S. Drug Enforcement Administration. Archived from the original on January 18, 2006. Retrieved February 13, 2010.

4   "Index Solutions: Emerging Markets Index," MSCI, https://www.msci.com/our-solutions/indexes/emerging-markets.

5   "Intentional Homicides (per 100,000 people)—Colombia," The World Bank Data, https://data.worldbank.org/indicator/VC.IHR.PSRC.P5.

6   "Former Colombia President Álvaro Uribe on Latin America's Journey to Political and Economic Security," Knowledge at Wharton, May 4, 2011, https://knowledge.wharton.upenn.edu/article/former-colombia-

president-alvaro-uribe-on-latin-americas-journey-to-political-and-economic-security/.

7   Michael Shifter, "Plan Colombia: A Retrospective," *Americas Quarterly*, July 18, 2012, https://www.americasquarterly.org/fulltextarticle/plan-colombia-a-retrospective/).

8   William C. Rempel, "How Colombia Is Busting Drug Cartels," CNN, January 18, 2012, https://www.cnn.com/2012/01/18/opinion/rempel-colombia-extradite-cartels/index.html.

9   "Colombia Foreign Direct Investment 1970–2021," Macrotrends, https://www.macrotrends.net/countries/COL/colombia/foreign-direct-investment.

10 "USAID Assistance For Plan Colombia," USAID, https://www.usaid.gov/news-information/fact-sheets/usaid-assistance-plan-colombia.

11   "New and Used Passenger Car and Light Truck Sales and Leases," Bureau of Transportation Statistics, https://www.bts.gov/content/new-and-used-passenger-car-sales-and-leases-thousands-vehicles.

12 Nelson Bocanegra and Julia Symmes Cobb, "After Decades of War, Colombia's FARC Rebels Debut Political Party," Reuters, August 27, 2017, https://www.reuters.com/article/us-colombia-peace-politics/after-decades-of-war-colombias-farc-rebels-debut-political-party-idUSKCN1B705U.

13 Ana Eiras and Brett Schaefer, "Argentina's Economic Crisis: An 'Absence of Capitalism,'" The Heritage Foundation, April 19, 2001, https://web.archive.org/web/20120119174030/http:/www.heritage.org/research/reports/2001/04/argentinas-economic-crisis-an-absence-of-capitalism.

14 World Economic Outlook database: April 2021, International Monetary Fund, https://www.imf.org/en/Publications/WEO/weo-database/2021/April/weo-report?c=512,914,612,614,311,213,911,314,193,122,912,313,419,513,316,913,124,339,638,514,218,963,616,223,516,918,748,618,624,522,622,156,626,628,228,924,233,632,636,634,238,662,960,423,935,128,611,321,243,248,469,253,642,643,939,734,644,819,172,132,646,648,915,134,652,174,328,258,656,654,336,263,268,532,944,176,534,536,429,433,178,436,136,343,158,439,916,664,826,542,967,443,917,544,941,446,666,668,672,946,137,546,674,676,548,556,678,181,867,6.org.

15   Michael Stott and Benedict Mander, "Argentina: How IMF's Biggest Ever Bailout Crumbled Under Macri," *Financial Times*, September 1, 2019, https://www.ft.com/content/5cfe7c34-ca48-11e9-a1f4-3669401ba76f.

16 "Most popular online retailers in Latin America." Statista, http://www.statista.com/statistics/321543/latin-america-online-retailer-visitors.

17 Mario Gabriele, "The Six Stories of Mercado Libre, *The Generalist*, May 16, 2021, https://www.readthegeneralist.com/briefing/meli.

18 Omri Wallach, "The World's Tech Giants, Compared to the Size of Economies," *Visual Capitalist*, July 7, 2021, https://www.visualcapitalist.com/the-tech-giants-worth-compared-economies-countries/.

19 Georgi Gotev, "Soft Drink Cold Chain Delivers Vaccines to Africa's Most Remote Corners," Euractiv, August 6, 2017, https://www.euractiv.com/section/health-consumers/news/soft-drink-cold-chain-delivers-vaccines-to-africas-most-remote-corners/.

20 "How We Work," Project Last Mile, https://www.projectlastmile.com/.

21 "Dam Burst at Mining Site Devastates Brazilian Town," *Aljazeera*, November 6, 2015, https://www.aljazeera.com/news/2015/11/6/dam-burst-at-mining-site-devastates-brazilian-town.

22 Samantha Pearson, Luciana Magalhaes, and Patricia Kowsmann, "Brazil's Vale Vowed 'Never Again.' Then Another Dam Collapsed," *Wall Street Journal*, December 31, 2019, https://www.wsj.com/articles/brazils-vale-vowed-never-another-dam-collapse-then-an-even-worse-one-11577809114.

23 "Vale Dam Disaster: $7bn Compensation for Disaster Victims," BBC News, https://www.bbc.com/news/business-55924743.

24 "Investor Pressure and the Global Tailings Review," Earthworks, https://earthworks.org/campaigns/preventing-mine-waste-disasters/investor-pressure-and-the-global-tailings-review/.

25 Paula Laier, "Vale Stock Plunges after Brazil Disaster; $19 Billion in Market Value Lost," Reuters, January 28, 2019, https://www.reuters.com/article/us-vale-sa-disaster-stocks/vale-stock-plunges-after-brazil-disaster-19-billion-in-market-value-lost-idUSKCN1PM1JP.

26 "Investor Pressure," Earthworks.

27 Ibid.

28 Philip Reeves, "What A New Constitution Could Mean For Chile," NPR, May 27, 2021, https://www.npr.org/2021/05/27/1000991508/many-in-the-group-writing-chiles-constitution-are-new-to-politics.

29 OECD Better Life Index (OECD), https://www.oecdbetterlifeindex.org/#/11111111111.

30 Some of the questions on the survey, such as "How often do you recite prayers?" and "How often do you practice meditation?" render this survey unrelatable to certain cultures; however, the premise that measures other than GDP are useful for evaluating the success of a country remains.

31 Lincoln Ando, "A Look Into Brazil's Booming Fintech Scene," *Forbes*, August 9, 2021, https://www.forbes.com/sites/forbestechcouncil/2021/08/09/a-look-into-brazils-booming-fintech-scene/?sh=1ec1342172b0.

32 "Country Commercial Guide—Brazil—Fintech," International Trade Administration, https://www.trade.gov/country-commercial-guides/brazil-fintech.

Chapter 9

1   Statement by His Excellency Dr. Hage G. Geingob, President of the Republic of Namibia, at the Genearl Debate of the 74th Session of the United Nations General Assembly, September 25, 2019, https://www.un.int/namibia/sites/www.un.int/files/Namibia/Statements/UNGA74 STATEMENTS/statement_by_h.e_president_geingob_unga74_25_september_2019_final.pdf.

2   Paheja Siririka, "Geingos, Theofelus Among 100 Most Influential Women," New Era, August 21, 2020, https://neweralive.na/posts/geingos-theofelus-among-100-most-influential-women.

3   Caroline Lim and Beryl Chu, "Female Executives in Asia Pacific: Women Hold Up Half the Sky," Pedersen and Partners, https://www.pedersenandpartners.com/news/female-executives-asia-pacific-women-hold-half-sky.

4   M. Tsui, "The Only Child and Educational Opportunity for Girls in Urban China," *Gender and Society* 16, no. 1 (2002): 74–92.

5   Jeff Grabmeier, "Having Fewer Children Reduced the Education Gap in China," Ohio State News, February 12, 2020, https://news.osu.edu/having-fewer-children-reduced-the-education-gap-in-china/.

6   "China Allows Three Children in Major Policy Shift," BBC News, May 31, 2021, https://www.bbc.com/news/world-asia-china-57303592.

7   "The Middle East's Power Business Women 2021," *Forbes,* https://www.forbesmiddleeast.com/lists/the-middle-east-power-businesswomen-2021/rania-nashar/.

8   "Small Change, Big Changes: Women and Microfinance," International Labour Office, https://www.ilo.org/wcmsp5/groups/public/@dgreports/@gender/documents/meetingdocument/wcms:091581.pdf.

9   "For Women in India, Small Loans Have a Big Impact," International Finance Corporation, October 2018, https://www.ifc.org/wps/wcm/connect/news_ext_content/ifc_external_corporate_site/news+and+events/news/india-microfinance-loans-rural-women.

10 Sugato Chakravarty, S. M. Zahid Iqbal, and Abu Zafar M. Shahriar, "Are Women 'Naturally' Better Credit Risks in Microcredit? Evidence from Field Experiments in Patriarchal and Matrilineal Societies in Bangladesh," American Economic Association.

11 Ashley Bittner and Brigette Lau, "Women-Led Startups Received Just 2.3% of VC Funding in 2020," *Harvard Business Review*, February 25, 2021, https://hbr.org/2021/02/women-led-startups-received-just-2-3-of-vc-funding-in-2020.

12 Allyson Kapin, "10 Stats That Build the Case for Investing in Women-Owned Startups," *Forbes,* January 28, 2019, https://www.forbes.com/sites/

allysonkapin/2019/01/28/10-stats-that-build-the-case-for-investing-in-women-led-startups/?sh=56f2855559d5.

13 "Globally, Countries Lose $160 Trillion in Wealth Due to Earnings Gaps Between Men and Women," World Bank, May 30, 2018, https://www.worldbank.org/en/news/press-release/2018/05/30/globally-countries-lose-160-trillion-in-wealth-due-to-earnings-gaps-between-women-and-men.

14 Chloe Taylor, "Female Leaders May Boost Share Price," CNBC, October 14, 2019, https://www.cnbc.com/2019/10/14/female-leaders-may-boost-share-price-performance-credit-suisse-says.html.

15 "CS Gender 300 Report Shows One Fifth of Board Positions Globally Now Held by Women," press release, Credit Suisse, October 10, 2019, https://www.credit-suisse.com/about-us-news/en/articles/media-releases/cs-gender-3000-report-shows-one-fifth-of-board-positions-globall-201910.html.

16 "Firms with More Female Executives 'Perform Better,'" BBC News, July 27, 2020, https://www.bbc.com/news/business-53548704.

17 Women-Led Businesses Are More Profitable Than Those Headed by Men - Here's Why," VNExplorer, https://vnexplorer.net/?#women-led-businesses-are-more-profitable-than-those-headed-by-men-heres-why-er2021436923.html.

18 "Asian Companies with More Women on Boards Deliver Better Results," India Times, June 27, 2019, https://economictimes.indiatimes.com/markets/stocks/news/asian-companies-with-more-women-on-boards-deliver-better-results/articleshow/69976337.cms.

19 "Growing Economies through Gender Parity," Council on Foreign Relations, https://www.cfr.org/womens-participation-in-global-economy/.

20 "Alternative Report on Thailand's Implementation in Compliance with the Convention on the Elimination of All Forms of Discrimination against Women (CEDAW) by the National Human Rights Commission of Thailand," United Nations Human Rights Treaty Bodies, https://tbinternet.ohchr.org/Treaties/CEDAW/SharedDocuments/THA/INT_CEDAW_IFN_THA_27198_E.pdf.

21 Womentum 2020, BofA Research p. 6.

22 "Women in Business and Management: Gaining Momentum in Latin America and the Caribbean," International Labour Office, May 2017, https://www.ilo.org/wcmsp5/groups/public/---ed_dialogue/---act_emp/documents/publication/wcms:579085.pdf.

23 John Levesque, "For Large U.S. Companies, CEOs Named John Outnumber Total Number of Woman CEOs," Seattle Business Magazine, May 2018, https://seattlebusinessmag.com/workplace/large-us-companies-ceos-named-john-outnumber-total-number-woman-ceos.

24 Leah Rodriguez, "7 Obstacles to Girls' Education and How to Overcome Them," Global Citizen, September 24, 2019, https://www.globalcitizen. org/en/content/barriers-to-girls-education-around-the-world/.

25 "Early Gender Bias," AAUW, https://www.aauw.org/issues/education/gender-bias/.

26 Womentum 2020, BofA Research, p. 7.

27 Ibid., pp. 8–9.

28 David Abney and Arancha González Laya, "This Is Why Women Must Play a Greater Role in the Global Economy," World Economic Forum, January 24, 2018, https://www.weforum.org/agenda/2018/01/this-is-why-women-must-play-a-greater-role-in-the-global-economy/#:~:text= Empowering%20women%20to%20participate%20equally%20in%20 the%20global,budget%20to%20education%2C%20health%2C% 20and%20nutrition%20than%20men.

29 "A New Generation: 25 Years of Efforts for Gender Equality in Education," UNESCO, https://unesdoc.unesco.org/ark:/48223/pf0000374514,pp. 9, 13–14.

30 Melanie Hanson, "College Enrollment & Student Demographic Statistics," Education Data Initiative, January 22, 2021, https://educationdata.org/college-enrollment-statistics.

31 Why Women-Owned Startups Are a Better Bet (bcg.com).

32 Jael Goldfine, "Why Richard Branson Gave 23andMe Billions to Go Public," Business of Business, February 11, 2021, https://www.businessof-business.com/articles/23andme-dna-testing-richard-branson-merger/.

33 Erin Griffith, "Houzz Worth $4 Billion in New Funding Round," *Forbes*, June 8, 2017, https://fortune.com/2017/06/08/houzz-worth-4-billion-in-new-funding-round/.

34 "Madam C.J. Walker," National Women's History Museum, https://www.womenshistory.org/education-resources/biographies/madam-cj-walker.

35 Michal Lev-Ram, "The Pandemic Cramped Rent the Runway's Style— But Here's How the Company Is Fashioning a Comeback in 2021," *Fortune*, December 24, 2020, https://fortune.com/2020/12/24/the-pandemic-cramped-rent-the-runways-style-but-heres-how-the-company-is-fashioning-a-comeback-in-2021/.

36 Sallie Krawcheck, "The Best Career Advice Women Are Not Getting," LinkedIn, May 16, 2016, https://www.linkedin.com/pulse/best-career-advice-women-getting-sallie-krawcheck/.

37 Maura McAdam, Caren Crowley, and Richard T. Harrison, "Digital Girl: Cyberfeminism and the Emancipatory Potential of Digital Entrepreneurship in Emerging Economies," *Small Business Economics* 55 (2020): 349–362.

38 Seema Chaturvedi, "Why We Need More Women Investing in Women," *Forbes*, March 9, 2021, https://www.forbes.com/sites/forbesfinance

council/2021/03/09/why-we-need-more-women-investing-in-women/?sh=6c80727c2557.

39 Alexandra Topping, "Companies with Female Leaders Outperform Those Dominated by Men, Data Shows," *The Guardian*, March 6, 2022, https://www.theguardian.com/business/2022/mar/06/companies-with-female-leaders-outperform-those-dominated-by-men-data-shows.

40 Allyson Kapin, "10 Stats That Build the Case."

41 Jesse Klein, "Women in Sustainability on Starting Their Careers and Making Change," *GreenBiz*, August 17, 2020, https://www.greenbiz.com/article/women-sustainability-starting-their-careers-and-making-change.

Conclusion

1   "Of the top 30 nations by revenue from digital services as a share of gross domestic product, 16 are in the emerging world," as Sharma pointed out in the *Financial Times*.

2   Euben Paracuelles, "How Is Technology Transforming Global Emerging Markets?" Nomura, April 2018, https://www.nomuraconnects.com/focused-thinking-posts/how-will-technology-transform-global-emerging-markets/.

Acknowledgments

I am deeply grateful to the many artists and quants who made this book happen. In particular, my editor, John Paine, offered instrumental support with his pragmatic, sensible, and clever wit coupled with his relentless drive for excellence. In addition, Lez Berdon, my assistant, solved some of the most difficult riddles I could dream up, finding contacts and delivering interviews from around the globe with nothing but a hint. To you both, thank you for your inexorable support.

Thank you to my delightful literary agent, Alice Martel. She encouraged me to shoot for the stars and settle for nothing less. I also want to thank my publisher, Bill Falloon at Wiley, and his excellent staff, for their help and support.

Lavish thanks are due to those who made instrumental contributions and whose ideas made it into the book in various ways, including Chris Pinney, Metu Osele, Brynn Mahnke, Jasmine Cochran, Simron Waskar, and my valued colleagues at the UUA. In addition, I must thank the research analysts who traveled the world alongside me and opened my eyes to the wonderous breadth of opportunity: Abhijit Kukreja, Ahmed Badr, Colin Miller, David Aserkoff, David Greyson, Gary Lo, Issam Ayari, Josh Meyers, Larry Speidell, Marcy Elkind, Marius Dan, Michael Daoud, and Simon Mandel.

I offer deep gratitude to my former colleagues who share my passion for economic development through innovative means and who helped me develop the ideas in this book: John Chisholm, who took a risk on me and taught me more than he will ever know, as well as Gary Bergstrom, Brian Wolahan, Ron Frashure, Churchill Franklin, Ted Noon, Renee Hoffman, and Bryan Carter.

Special thanks to the families who took me into their homes and brought me into their lives. To the Bhandari family, the Farah family, and the Minev family; thank you. Thank you as well to Jill and Dragos Ilie, John and Michael O'Leary, and Sudha and Prem Garg whose gifts from afar were invaluable.

I am of course deeply indebted to all the people whose research and commentary are cited in the book. Thank you for your thoughtful teachings.

Finally, I wish to thank my family for putting up with me during this intensive, wild adventure. In particular, my parents, Paulette and Jay Mehta, who read and edited endless rewrites of stories that they themselves inspired. Also, my husband and children, Nikhil, Jasper, Griffen, and Zara, who displayed extreme grace, patience, and encouragement. I could not be more grateful for your support.

About the Author

Asha Mehta, CFA, is the Founder and Chief Investment Officer of Global Delta Capital. Her thematic focus includes Emerging & Frontier Markets and Sustainable Investing.

Previously, she was an investment banker at Goldman Sachs and Lead Portfolio Manager and Director of Responsible Investing at Acadian Asset Management. Early in her career, she conducted microfinance lending in India. She has traveled to over 80 countries and lived in six.

Asha is a market maker and investment pioneer. She managed the world's first Frontier markets fund as well as the first institutional actively managed Emerging Markets Fossil Fuel Free fund. She launched one of the earliest onshore China strategies in the United States. Separately, Asha led the first quantitative investor to become a signatory to the United Nations' Principles for Responsible Investing, which now oversees more than $100 trillion in investment assets.

Asha was named one of the Top 10 Women in Asset Management by Money Management Executive and profiled as a "Brilliant Quant" by *Forbes* magazine. Asha is an active advocate of financial literacy and financial empowerment. She is a supporter of several related organizations, including Compass Working Capital and 100 Women in Finance.

Asha holds an MBA with Honors from The Wharton School, University of Pennsylvania, and a B.S., Biological Sciences, and A.B., Anthropology, from Stanford University. She lives between Boston and Florida with her husband, two young boys, and baby girl.

Index